PLUNGE2POVERTY

PLUNGE2POVERTY

An Intensive Poverty Simulation Experience

Jimmy and Janet Dorrell

NEW HOPE
PUBLISHERS

Birmingham, Alabama

New Hope® Publishers
P. O. Box 12065
Birmingham, AL 35202-2065
www.newhopepublishers.com

Library of Congress Cataloging-in-Publication Data

Dorrell, Jimmy, 1950-
  Plunge2poverty : an intensive poverty simulation experience / Jimmy
and Janet Dorrell.
     p. cm.
  ISBN 978-1-59669-087-5 (sc)
  1. Poverty--Religious aspects--Christianity. 2. Christian
education--Activity programs. I. Dorrell, Janet, 1957- II. Title.
BV4647.P6D67 2006
261.8'325--dc22
                            2006038601

ISBN-10: 1-59669-087-9
ISBN-13: 978-1-59669-087-5

N074138 • 0507 • 5M1

ENDORSEMENTS

"Without a doubt, this experience is something every North American youth worker should provide for their students."
—*Will Penner, Executive Editor for* The Journal of Student Ministries

"This is one book that will be critical for every student minister to have in their library."
—*Johnny L. Derouen, PhD, Associate Professor of Student Ministry, Southwestern Baptist Theological Seminary*

Other books by Jimmy Dorrell

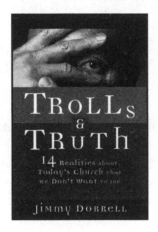

Trolls & Truth:
14 Realities About Today's Church
That We Don't Want to See

DEDICATION

This book is dedicated to the poor of our world: the 1.4 billion people who live each day without the basic necessities of life, and the parents of some 30,000 children, who watch helplessly each day as these children die from preventable hunger-related causes. No simulation will ever come close to recreating the pain and frustration that the poor experience every day.

C O N T E N T S

SECTION 1
PLUNGE2POVERTY START

SECTION 2

PLUNGE2POVERTY FINISH

SECTION 3

PLUNGE2POVERTY SIMULATION TOOLS

Acknowledgments

While statistics and photos can crystallize the dilemma of hunger and poverty in our minds, the real experience is unimaginable for most of us.

Can you imagine what life would be like if you were a parent watching your malnourished child slowly die? What if there were food and medicine readily available that would heal your child, but you were never able to buy?

What would it feel like to be a middle-aged worker recently diagnosed with an incurable mental disorder or HIV/AIDS, and watch your family gradually fear and disown you, with the streets as your only option?

How desperate would you feel if you were to experience real hunger pains so intense that you became lifeless, and immobilized, thinking death your only consolation?

Poverty affects almost half the world, and 1.4 billion human beings live in "absolute poverty," meaning they live without the basic necessities to survive. Yet many of us have only missed a meal due to a diet or personal choice, not for lack of access. The division between the "have's" and "have-not's" is wide and neither group probably understands the other very well. But to ignore the chasm is irresponsible and certainly not Christ-like.

We who have committed our lives to follow the God who fed the masses, healed the sick, cast out the demonic forces, and forgave the sinner must be willing to follow our Lord's reminder: When we feed, heal, visit, and give a drink of water, we do it to Him (Matthew 25:37–40).

Without a doubt, Janet and I never expected to live out this journey among the poor and marginalized. Like most middle-class Christians, we grew up personally disconnected from those who live life day-to-day, unsure of their next meal or dollar. We gave our money and canned goods when the church asked and occasionally remembered the poor in a prayer or service project. But we did not direct our paths. It was God who brought us together and who shaped our journey. He, who called each of us to compassion among the poor, gently led us from apathy to involvement.

With each forward step, God has shown us new insights about our own selfishness and blindness to others' sorrows. With each backward step, we still could not drown out the clarion call to incarnate connection with the broken and struggling people of our city, nation, and world. Through experiences, Bible study, late-night discussions, and prayer, we recognize that the Father has shaped our lives in ways we never imagined.

This book is a compilation of our more than 28 years of life and learning among the poor. We have learned that poverty is harsh and unfair. We have worked in the slums of Calcutta, hugged physically and mentally disabled orphans in Mexico City, and drilled water wells in a small village of Haiti. In our own city, we have lived among the poor, experienced church with the homeless, and played a thousand games of freeze-tag with inner-city children. These are our heroes, names you will never hear or know. They are the ones God used to teach us how to see life differently.

We recognize the joyful tapestry in ministry with family in all of this: Our marriage of 30 years is unlike most unions, but close because of the narrow road God has given us to walk. Our four children, Seth, Josh, Zach, and Christy, have been reared in a neighborhood and taken to places in the world unlike what most children experience. It has been with such a deep sense of gratitude to God that we have watched our children embrace their unique upbringing and thank us for those tough choices we made to live on tougher streets; to have racially, economically, and socially diverse visitors; and to choose a lifestyle that expresses some consistency with the needs of the poor. We are grateful for their decisions.

Each of our oldest boys, now married, has chosen to live and work among the poor. Our younger children have befriended "outcasts" and snubbed affluent lifestyles. They have joined us when we've trained other youth in the Poverty Simulation, often giving up their weekends to help cook, sweep, and share their own stories from the neighborhood and world. Their openness to what matters in life, their faith, and their joy bring us a deep sense of what it means to be a family with a purpose.

We recognize that it has been the response of the participants experiencing the simulation during these 20 years that has most encouraged us. For each one that received a spark of enthusiasm to go back home and get involved or go to a poor country on a missions trip, we reaped the joy when they told us how the training inspired them. We are thankful for each letter or note that God has used to clearly affirm that He uses this Poverty Simulation experience to transform lives.

Perhaps the most important unsung heroes are the youth and college directors and sponsors who have traveled, sometimes at great distances, to bring their groups of students to experience the Poverty Simulation. It sometimes has been hard for leaders to convince the parents of affluent children that their kids would be poor for a few days; to suggest to church staff that something is needed as an alternative to other trends in student ministry; and to learn how to process when everyone returned home to real life   after the Poverty Simulation.

Finally, we thank New Hope Publishers for their venture to offer this guidebook that is outside the standard lessons. New Hope's encouragement, professionalism, and genuine concern for us and the churches and individuals they serve are rewarding.

Jimmy and Janet Dorrell

P2P Testimonial

Poverty Simulation Leader's Testimony

Clinton Lowin, Senior High pastor,
The Chapel in North Canton, Ohio

I am the senior high youth pastor, and we were trying to organize some programs for the summer. Instead of doing the normal trip to the amusement park, we changed our plans. We decided the Poverty Simulation would be the wake-up call for our students and adults to understand the need for sensitivity to the down-and-outs, and needy people of the world. The weekend was awesome. Even the local newspaper (The Canton Repository) *followed us throughout the weekend to record the story. The name of Christ was proclaimed, students were changed, and other churches are wanting to know more about how to do it. Our students will never be the same.*

P2P Testimonial

Poverty Simulation Participant's Testimony

Brittany Rasmussen Mackey, Atlanta, Georgia

I took a civic education class about poverty at Baylor to avoid a physical education class. I had no idea it would change my life! Not only was I unaware of the scope of poverty in my own community, but came to understand its reality in America and the world. The Poverty Simulation was required in that class and it rocked my world. Because of it, I changed my goals and moved into a lower-income neighborhood in Atlanta to teach struggling children. Today I run an urban ministry and am so thankful for what I learned through the challenging experience.

Foreword

What It Is: An Intensive Poverty Simulation Experience

In 1986, a minister of youth called us, "I need help!" This minister was a sharp seminary graduate who had invested a couple of years into his student group. Its members were exemplary young people in so many ways: They were intelligent, had strong self-images, and were churchgoing Christians. But the minister had discovered that, behind the appearance of their faith, there was a strong prejudice against other people groups, cultures, and the poor. There was racism, ethnocentrism, and pretentiousness. The Bible verses the youth had memorized apparently had not penetrated all the layers of preconceived stereotypes that their middle-class minds had adopted.

Jimmy and I had just returned to the United States from India where we had served during a three-month, short-term mission with World Hunger Relief, a Christian organization committed to community and economic development. Before the India placement, we experienced three months of training in Haiti. By the end of the six-month commitment, we had witnessed some of the world's worst poverty. Our own worldview had been changed as we considered, *How do we live responsibly in our own culture, knowing that thousands of children die each day from preventable illnesses that are hunger related?* We were trying to make sense of our own vocational call.

The phone call from the minister of youth was timely. "Yes! We can help because we understand more than ever the paradox of wealthy Christians living in a world of need, and not seeming to care about those needs." And so we did. The first Poverty Simulation was designed for that minister's group of young people and the impact it had on them was surprising to all of us. Somehow, God used a weekend experience to awaken a group of students and to sensitize them to hear God's voice above and beyond their cultural biases and imaginations. They went home committed to making a difference in their community and world.

Results

The intensive experience of the Poverty Simulation had such a dramatic impact on the minister of youth that he wrote an article for a youth worker magazine. Before long, another student group contacted Jimmy and me and booked the same weekend experience. Like a fire, word began to spread among student workers and, over the next year, many more leaders connected with various denominations began to call.

As the Poverty Simulation experience format continued to mature, we found a building site and set scheduled, specific weekends to receive up to 75 students at a time. Each weekend experience humbled us because of what God did in the lives of so many students.

Looking back more than 20 years now, the Poverty Simulation has trained more than 6,000 students to understand a theme that is basic to Christian discipleship: being concerned about "the least" (Matthew 25:40). Student and adult groups have come from some ten states to plunge to poverty for a weekend. The experience has even been modified to help six groups other than ours, with sites across the nation, to offer a Poverty Simulation experience.

Perhaps the most profound joy as a result of these two decades comes from reading the heartfelt communication in the letters of former Poverty Simulation participants, who have written to say, "That weekend changed my life!"

Literally. Some of the college students who attended a simulation eventually changed their majors. Others chose an urban ministry internship as a next step. Several went on missions trips to developing countries. Many began to rearrange their spending patterns. Still others simply came to acknowledge that they had played religion for years, but had never previously understood the joy of submitting their lives—even their money, power, and dreams—to the God who cares for the whole world.

Transferable Concepts: You Can Do It Too!

Through these 20-plus years, we have been asked to help others replicate what has become an important tool, in order to create an environment in which God can gently confront His followers with the sinful by-products of an affluent culture. Groups from Washington, D.C., to North Carolina, to Oklahoma have taken the core principles and basic components provided herein to create their own Poverty Simulations. Some have closely followed our model, while others have rearranged many of the elements to fit their particular learning situations.

Our goal is simply to provide guidance from what we have learned through delivering this experience to thousands of youth, young adult college students, and adults.

While you may not be an expert in global economics or worldviews, the resources you need to lead an effective Poverty Simulation experience are here. This book will be a substantial guide as you plan. Yet nothing will replace a personal experience of attending someone else's simulation first.

We have observed that the best P2P leaders and facilitators are those who have experienced the training personally, without controlling the circumstances in their local context. Feel free to connect with Mission Waco's Web site www.missionwaco. org or other groups referenced in this book and see when the next available P2P fits your schedule so you can participate.

P2P Testimonial

Poverty Simulation Leader's Testimony

Cody Schimelpfenig, Community Development director, Urban Homeworks, Inc., Minneapolis, Minnesota

The "street weekend" we did last month was a huge success, in that it really shook up those who participated, including me. The participants were young adults (23–33 years old) who are urban dwellers, so city life is not new. But . . . seeing the plight of those who are homeless up close and personal was a new experience. It really broke people's hearts, as it should. It challenged the charity mentality many have come out of as Christians and showed them the need for social justice, which forces one to look at the bigger picture of why homelessness exists, what political decisions have been/are being made here that directly impact this population, and so on. For many of these young believers that is a new paradigm.

Again, thanks for sharing your mission and model with others. It is bearing fruit for the Lord.

Introduction

How do you disciple a culture of "Rich Young Rulers"?

"That's me," the young man announced. "I'm the rich young ruler who is too afraid to leave all my stuff and follow Jesus," he sobbed almost uncontrollably to one of the student leaders. "I'm a rich kid who never missed a meal, bought everything I ever wanted, and have not given even one dollar to the poor. I'm selfish and spoiled and I know it."

Over the next half hour, the honor student and football star broke in and out of tears as he confessed his struggle with material possessions and desire to live consistently with his faith. "Am I going to hell because I haven't sold my stuff and given it to the poor to follow Jesus? What am I supposed to do?"

Most of this young man's peers, who were in the room and listening, knew exactly what he was talking about and a little of his feelings. They finally had begun to understand how materialism and privilege had shaped their young lives. Most did not like what they now saw in themselves, in light of their experience that night in the Poverty Simulation.

Across the room, the student director, who had enlisted the young man to come to the simulation, quietly smiled and prayed for God to do a new work in this kid's life. The director recognized this crisis of faith and knew that this was desperately needed, in order for the young, natural leader to become a supernatural follower. The question at hand was a question of allegiance and lordship that almost all suburbanite youth and young adults must face if they are going to take their faith in Christ seriously. The question is: In a culture of affluence, what does it mean to follow Jesus?

A clash of values

The "rich young ruler" (Matthew 19:16–30) asked Jesus this same, important question in a similar way: "How do I get eternal life?" he implored. Hearing from the Lord that obedience to the commandments is important in the spiritual journey, the rich young ruler found great satisfaction in his supposed accomplishments of the Decalogue. Although, we know from the Sermon on the Mount that he probably had not obeyed them, based on Jesus's deeper interpretation! But knowing that there might be more to this important question, he garnered the courage to ask, "What do I still lack?" (v. 20)

What a great question! If we can encourage a generation of young Christians to be open enough to ask the very same question, our churches can become more mature. Unfortunately, many young Christians today are pretentious enough to think they understand life and do not need anyone telling them "what they lack." Power, affluence, and a sense of entitlement have created a seemingly closed-value system and has dulled the courage of "followers" to seek and ask. Yet discipleship definitely requires that we ask the Teacher to expose in us what we still lack.

But not only do we rarely ask what we still lack, we also have allowed many of our own non-Christian cultural values to be "Christianized." Instead of recognizing them as pagan values as Jesus did in the sermon, we somehow have enmeshed opposing values into a syncretistic pot. How often have you heard sermons preached on spending too much on clothing or food or worrying about tomorrow? Instead, I observe that US Christians often acknowledge the designer label, affirm the expensive sports car, or spend more time talking about stocks, bonds, and mutual funds than the kingdom of God. Why do we recreate God in our likeness, rather than recognize that we are created in His image?

Jesus's conclusion

Jesus's answer was more than this other young man could bear. "Go, sell your possessions and give to the poor, and you will have treasure in heaven. Then, come, follow me" (Matthew 19: 21). Though he had the courage to ask, the young ruler was not prepared for the intense responsibility to God's kingdom. "When the young man heard this, he went away sad, because he had great wealth." And Jesus said, "I tell you the truth, it is hard for a rich man to enter the kingdom of heaven." (v. 23)

If even Jesus's disciples asked in astonishment, "Who then can be saved?" we also must ask more about this difficult teaching, for many of us are clearly rich, certainly more than the rich young ruler of that day. If our wealth, like the young ruler's, can be more of a spiritual handicap—rather than a supposed privilege or blessing—should not some of our Christian teaching among the most affluent youth-culture in history cause them to ask that question: What do I still lack?

Not entertainment discipleship

Leading a middle-income youth, college, or young adult group toward biblical discipleship is no easy task today. Competing opportunities abound for most groups to enjoy scores of activities: concerts, sports camps, travel, or a personal room full of the latest electronics and accessories. There are even "competing" churches that offer bigger and better events to lure the local participants away to a more sensationalized event or activity.

Even committed students, who attend a local Christian group, may be only partially engaged with the program that a director has spent hours planning in hopes of building spiritual maturity. Add to that parents' and the other church or parachurch staff members' expectations of the students and there seems to be more confusion as to how to lead today's young believers. There are times in every student or adult director's ministry when he or she wonders what the fringe stuff has to do with following Jesus.

Many seasoned student workers have discovered that, beyond the entertainment, T-shirts, and push for growing attendance, there are students who are looking for something deeper; something that will give them a sense of purpose beyond the normal lifestyle to which they have become accustomed. Many of these students know only a little about the Bible and consider it part of an old, foreign culture that seems to offer few common connections with today's world. They may wonder, *What do bath robed-looking disciples on donkeys have to say to a hip-hop generation that drives the latest cars?*

These new generations of youth long for a cause bigger than themselves. They want a faith that challenges them to sacrifice and make a difference. Many of them lie down at night wondering whether or not their belief in God really means anything more than a ticket to heaven after they have lived "the good life."

Service projects are not enough

Any discipleship leader who works with students knows that classroom-style Bible studies usually are poorly attended or underappreciated by activity-driven youth and young adults. Many leaders have turned to "service learning," creating work projects that have substance for their groups.

There are many worthy causes that student directors have found to help engage youth. Painting the house of a low-income elderly person, cleaning trash from vacant lots, leading a backyard Bible club, and other projects help students get their hands dirty and feel more involved. Summer missions trips to other countries, metropolitan centers, or rural areas add to the sense of awakening that so often is needed. Based on those experiences, many students begin to ask deeper questions as human need and their own comfortable lifestyles back home confront their views.

As important as these activities are, there is still the risk that many of the students will revel in their good works and never ask the harder questions, as the rich young ruler asked, about the purpose served by a project or about how it affects one's faith. If painting the house or playing with poor children becomes nothing more than an activity, there is the real danger of reinforcing privilege, rather than engaging in a transformational lifestyle in order to be more conformed to the image of Christ.

How then do we teach this transformational lifestyle? How do we create an atmosphere where students have the courage to ask, "Is there more I still lack?" The answer is to present the greater challenge of discipleship, to engage students in activities that take away their privilege, control, and power. It is only as they are stripped of their ability to "fix the world" or "own the world" that they face themselves and the inner core of who they are and what they believe. It was only as Jesus's young disciples tried to heal and failed to do so that they became truly teachable.

Overcoming personal ego, pride, and power may come from a Bible study, discipleship manual, or service project. But we know without a doubt that God takes those empty, helpless moments in our lives—when we see the ugliness of our own sin and the depth of our dependence on Him—and uses them to encourage us to submit to His transforming will.

Lost and found—shaping attitudes

Jesus wisely lists the first "Beatitude" for entrance into heaven as the one we dislike most: "Blessed are the poor in spirit, for theirs is the kingdom of heaven" (Matthew 5:3). Spiritual poverty is a prerequisite for spiritual maturity. Our pride, arrogance, and independence thwart teachableness. So the Teacher often must bring us to a place of humility before we can grow.

God does this humbling work of breaking us in different ways. He can use a health problem, family break up, financial loss, death of a loved one, natural disaster, and other personal crises as gateways to transformation and deeper discipleship. He is not dependent on our church or parachurch programs to do what ultimately only He can do. Yet even in those difficult circumstances He allows, many people may never humble themselves to Him without an experience such as the Poverty Simulation.

How to create an environment for humility

As in this intensive Poverty Simulation experience, God also can use mentors or programs as agents of change. He can help you to create environments that may provide ground where His Spirit can do His good work in those with whom we work.

Our goal as disciple-makers is to find ways that followers of Jesus can be confronted, as was the rich young ruler, and built up spiritually. Although we can create an environment for more sensitive asking and listening, we cannot make anyone ask the question, "What do I still lack?" And we certainly cannot predict the Lord's answer or demand of them.

There is no one tool that works to create this environment for all students, but the set of tools in this Poverty Simulation experience and similar experiences do have critical components that have proven timely and instructive.

There are at least seven key components for any designed Christian-training experience, in order to confront the impact of affluence in our culture of "rich young rulers." The Poverty Simulation has incorporated these components successfully into its activities to yield significant impact on students who attend. The key components are:

1. Awareness—The harsh realities of poverty must be understood to help the students recognize the world as it really is, not as how they perceive the world to be.
2. Biblically based—God's call to the poor and marginalized must be understood as a basic mandate of Scripture, and not as an optional choice.
3. Intensity—The experience must be long enough to create personal discomfort and frustration, in order to expose the heart's deceits.
4. Reflection—The students must have ample opportunity to allow God's Spirit to reveal to them the darkness of their hearts so that they can see themselves more through His eyes.
5. Confession—Acknowledging personal selfishness, apathy,

and greed provides the next step to change.

6. Commitment and next steps—Understanding the cost and options and making a commitment to lifestyle changes based on these new convictions is critical.
7. Accountability—Change requires a community of encouragement over longer periods of time.

Each of these critical components to the Poverty Simulation will be discussed in-depth in the following chapters.

Plunge2Poverty!

P2P Testimonial

Poverty Simulation Leader's Testimony

"Middle Class Youth from First Mennonite in Kansas Become Homeless in Texas" Bev Regier, Newton, Kansas, wrote for Mennonite Church USA:

Rusty Bonham, the youth director, brought 27 youth to the sweltering heat of Waco, Texas, last summer to attend the Mission Waco Poverty Simulation. What struck most of them was how nice and generous the homeless on the streets were toward them. Upon their return to Newton, the youth continued the challenge by helping New Jerusalem Mission get a shelter open for the winter. "After the simulation, we realized we didn't want to be a youth group that keeps its doors locked."

P2P Testimonial

Poverty Simulation Leader's Testimony

John Mein, Calvary Baptist Church, Washington, D.C.

We had more than 250 youth each year go through the simulation that we learned about from you many years ago. We modified it to a 24-hour experience for our Urban Hands groups who came to help us in D.C. during spring break, summer, and at Christmas. I could fill a book of testimonies that came from the Poverty Simulation. Seeing the amount of change that takes place in such a short amount of time and how God used the experience to create such a servant-minded change has been awesome.

P2P Testimonial

Poverty Simulation Participant's Testimony

Phebe Braik, St. Louis, Missouri

I recently "Googled" your name and saw where you are still doing the Poverty Simulations. I am writing 12 years after I went through it there in Waco, Texas. I was in the group from Missouri. I just wanted to say thank you for the many ways that experience gave me lessons and insights. God really changed my heart, and I have never looked at giving in the same way since then. Through all those activities, I realized there are more important things in life than my momentary material things for a comfortable life. Thank you!

PLUNGE2POVERTY
START

Intensive Poverty Simulation Experience

Goals:

To challenge youth to become aware of local, national, and global poverty, and to understand what they can do to make a difference

To awaken their sense of privilege and responsibility to be involved, as kingdom followers, in the things that concern the King

To pair youths' loss of possessions, limited choices, and their encounters with the poor with challenging activities, videos, talks, and group time that address the barriers between the rich and the poor

Prepare to Take the Plunge

God can use each P2P leader as an agent of change as leaders yield to Him. He can help you to create environments that provide space where His Spirit will do His good work in those with whom you work.

Your goal as disciple-maker is to help provide ground where Jesus will confront youth—as He did the rich, young rulers—and build them up spiritually. Although you can create an environment for more sensitive spiritual reflection, you cannot make anyone ask the question, "What do I still lack?" And you certainly cannot predict the Lord's answer or demand of your youth. Thus, as leader, you must not only prepare practically; you want to prepare spiritually for this experience.

To best prepare, please read through this book before your P2P. You will want to pay special attention to the appendixes, including spending time with appendix 9, page 146, biblical references to the poor, and appendix 8, page 135, resources for content. You may wish to study additional references, including material regarding the community where you will conduct your P2P: its people, leaders, churches, and other information.

Prayer is key. It will be important for you to spend time in prayer for God's plans for each of your participants to hear His voice. We encourage you to enlist pray-ers, who will uphold you before, during, and after this simulation. As you encourage participants to do likewise, you will need to:

- Hear God's voice.
- Become aware of the harsh realities of poverty.

- Understand God's call to the poor and marginalized as a basic mandate of Scripture.
- Examine your heart.
- See yourself more through God's eyes.
- Confess any personal selfishness, apathy, and greed, in order to change.
- Commit to lifestyle changes based on new convictions.
- Be accountable over time to act on what you experience.

Facilitator training

To have a successful simulation experience, you will need facilitators who will commit to the P2P activity. You will need to gather your facilitators ahead of the Poverty Simulation for at least an hour-long training session. You may wish to provide each of them with this guidebook or at least copies of the reproducible materials herein. During training, share the P2P goal, overview for each day of the experience, and tasks facilitators can support, including each of the service opportunities show here.

Facilitators will have important responsibilities:

Greet and interact with parents and others who bring participants to the simulation.

Help gather and file permission forms and fees.

Collect and grade pretests and posttests.

Assist with setup and lockup at the clothing exchange on the first night and last day.

Monitor sleeping arrangements and assist with any "crowd control" or other security at your P2P site.

Know and reiterate guidelines to participants, as needed.

Coordinate, prepare, and serve meals, including the World Banquet fare, as well as Chance Cards and apples afterwards.

Act as processors during debriefing sessions with participants. (On Day 2, you will help students process what they are learning. You will need several debriefing processors. You will need to gather these processors together ahead of the simulation and simulate good processing techniques.)

Leader's key

This leader's key is designed to help you identify elements of the Poverty Simulation in the following pages and makes this guidebook easy to use as you conduct this experience.

Specific instructions for leaders' and facilitators' actions during each day's activities are in bold letters.
For example: **Because late entrances can have an impact on your group dynamics, you are encouraged not to begin instructions until everyone is present.**

Each day's simulation steps are identified with screened headlines:
For example: Prepare for powerlessness

Pages with important simulation guidelines and rules are noted with this street sign and the lane-line marker.

Items you will need are identified for each simulation day and noted with a checklist box.
For example: ☐ Watch

Sample dialogue and sections of dialogue with participants are identified with a shaded background.

For example: "Thank you all for coming to participate in this simulation experience. Each one of you, through your participation, is making a crucial commitment to learn about the poor and God's heart and mandates to us regarding them.

First Night Overview

What you will do:

Prepare for Powerlessness

Welcome and Pretest Participants

Flip the Script

Share the Facts

Give the guidelines

Answer a Few Questions

Let the Choices Begin

Shop 'Til Ya Drop

Bed, Bath, or Beyond

Items you will need for the first night

☐ Watch

☐ Release forms

☐ Participant fees (if applicable)

☐ Pretest (appendix 4, page oo) and pencils

☐ Numbered tickets (numbers on each end of ticket)
   and an empty can for collecting for homeless drawing

☐ Room in which participants can change clothes

☐ Space to lock up participants' valuables

☐ Used/well-worn shirts, pants, and shoes for a "thrift store
   closet" or access to a nearby thrift or secondhand store

☐ Numbered tickets for bed and breakfast assignments

Optional

☐ Extra lighting as needed

☐ Safety precautions as needed

General schedule

In this particular model, the event begins at 8:00 p.m. Friday
night and ends at 2:30 p.m. Sunday afternoon. You can adjust
this schedule to span a different shorter or longer P2P.

The first night sample schedule

Start time: 8:00 p.m.

Please note: Participants should have been told before the simulation commences that they are expected to remain in the simulation training from the beginning to the end, without leaving for any reason. If participants cannot do so, you will want to ask them to participate in the simulation at another time.

In approximately the first 45 minutes of the simulation:
- Welcome participants' arrival
- Collect release forms and file as participants arrive (appendix 3, page 104)
- Collect any fees
- Give the pretest and then collect it from participants
- Explain simulation rules

(Wait to explain simulation instructions until all participants have arrived.)

8:45

During the next approximately 15 minutes:
- Allow for a breakout time, in order for participants to choose the belongings they will keep with them during the simulation, and to allow participants to put away all of their other belongings.

9:00

In the next approximately 15 minutes:
- Allow participants to pick through and choose the worn clothing and shoes, in order to wear some secondhand clothing for the simulation.

11:30 Lights out

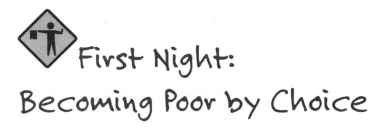

First Night: Becoming Poor by Choice

Prepare for powerlessness

In advance of the Plunge2Poverty you schedule, you are to tell students very little about what will happen during these days. They are to arrive promptly at a predetermined time for the simulation.

Though worried parents and supervisors may want to know all the details to be sure of the students' safety, it is important to keep the participants "in the dark" as much as is possible. Since powerlessness is a part of the poverty experience, the more the leader tells the students what they will experience, the more he or she empowers them with information that can give them opportunity to prepare. Though it is equally important not to deceive students to attend the simulation thinking it is something else, a simple explanation can be used.

For example: "All I can tell you is that you will become poor for the (simulation or simulation time-period)," should be enough.

Because late entrances can have an impact on your group dynamics, you are encouraged not to begin the instructions until everyone is present. Participants should have been told prior to the simulation that they are expected to be there from the beginning to the end of the training, and not to leave for any reason. If they cannot do so, have them participate at a different time. The uninterrupted intensity of the activities does have significant impact on the learning.

Before you explain all of the rules of the simulation,

you will want to collect all signed release forms and fees (see appendix 3, page 104). (Mission Waco charges $45 per participant to cover expenses.) **Release forms should be kept in a special place in case of some sickness or accident, and in case notes from parents regarding a participant's health condition need attention. A selected facilitator should be responsible for these forms.**

Welcome and pretest participants

Along with a general welcome, affirm each person's presence and commitment to come learn about the poor and God's heart and mandates regarding them.

For example: "Thank you all for coming to participate in this simulation experience. Each one of you, through your participation, is making a crucial commitment to learn about the poor and God's heart and mandates to us regarding them.

Before you share the actual guidelines for the simulation, hand out the written pretest (see appendix 4, page 106) for each participant to complete. The questions are difficult for most students and adults, who often are uninformed regarding the world in which they live. Many participants are unaware of poor people's plight in the United States or outside its borders. But the pretest questions help to engage participants and encourage them to begin to think about many of the critical issues ahead of them in the simulation (answer key, page 110).

These students have come from a world of stuff, busyness, fun, and preoccupation. Now the pretest asks them about hungry kids, other worldviews, and global economics. Slowly, in the silence of the pretest, participants are settling down into the reminder of a needy world. There is a daunting reality check that suggests the importance of this pending experience.

The pretest scores compared to the same assessment given as a posttest will be one indicator of what participants have learned cognitively throughout the simulation. While most of them may be unmotivated to engage deeply in a "test," particularly one that likely shows how little they know about their own world, it does become an important tool for the P2P leaders. You will be able to determine later how much they learned "on the way" in this experience rather than through formal teaching.

Flip the script

Creating role reversal in one hour is no easy task, but in effect this is the leader's goal. Most students who come from wealth generally have no idea of how poor people view the world or how poor people live each day. Middle-class youth usually exist with significant power and information that yields for them at least a sense of control. This role reversal and loss of power will be hard for them to experience. Yet, for this simulation, participants will be reminded constantly how this lack of control and information can be a key tool God uses, in order to teach them what they could not learn otherwise.

Most participants will have an insatiable desire to know the experience guidelines as quickly as possible. For them, knowledge is power. Almost before the facilitator can even explain the rules of the ensuing Poverty Simulation, students are demanding answers.

For example: "What does that mean?" "What are you going to do to us?" "Can we. . . ?" "What if. . . ?" "I have a right to know!"

And the flurry of questions may explode on the leader who is in the process of carefully unpacking the rules of the simulation. **Assure participants that most of their questions will be answered, but many of those questions that seek too much detail will be ignored.**

Share the facts

As simulation leader, you will announce an overview of the experience to come.

For example: "For one weekend (or other time period) you will simulate a designed experience that attempts to help you understand a bit of what poor people experience each day. Their poverty is real. It is important that each of you take them seriously and never mock the poor whose lives are frequently entangled in struggle and grief unlike any simulation can replicate. These are some of the facts.

(Read aloud each of the facts listed here.):
- Today, about 30,000 children in our world, who are younger than five years old, breathed their last breath because of hunger-related causes.
- Today, half the world's inhabitants made less than two US dollars.
- Today, over 1.4 billion people in our global village of 6.4 billion people live in "absolute poverty," a condition that describes those without even the basic necessities of life.
- Today, young teenage girls were sold as sex slaves to rich businessmen.
- Today, thousands of children spent 14 hours in a sweatshop, earning less than one US dollar.
- Today, the disease of AIDS killed thousands of parents, and their children are now orphans who must take care of themselves, with little support.
- Even today in your own country, some kids went hungry, others were physically abused, and millions could not see a doctor because they have no health insurance.

Today, you have the privilege of learning about those you may have ignored or forgotten. So, in the midst of these few days, care for them and listen to the Spirit of God, who can speak to you in this unique time of your life. This simulation could affect your whole life, especially if you invite God to change you!

Give the guidelines
Announce the following simulation rules to participants:

- Your brief time of poverty will simulate that of a low-income mother or father of three children, who lives on welfare in this state. You will have only the resources this mother or father would have.
- Throughout the experience, you will find yourself in some of the same dilemmas and having to make the same choices that the poor make every day.
- In a few minutes, you will be given a packet of "simulated welfare money" in the amount of $40.* This sum is the actual prorated amount that a parent on TANF (Temporary Assistance for Needy Families) would receive over the same given time that you are participating in the Poverty Simulation. You must make all your economic choices with that currency. No other form of monetary or material exchange is acceptable.
- You will buy your food with those dollars, pay rent, and purchase clothing. If there is an unforeseen crisis that occurs, for which you must make payment, you will have to meet that obligation with your available cash.

*The actual amount may change based on current Federal Poverty Guidelines and TANF benefits in your state. Other fees and expenses below may also be modified. Try to be current so that the impact is legitimate.

Besides those general guidelines, announce these specific rules participants are asked to follow:

1. You may keep only four items that you brought with you. Those four items include almost everything, such as sleeping bag, pillow, toothbrush, towel, toothpaste, clean clothes, Bible, books, CD players, and so on. All other items you brought (excluding the exceptions below) will be locked away for the rest of the simulation time and you

cannot have access to them until this simulation ends.

2. You must put away all jewelry, watches, cell phones, keys, knives, billfolds, purses—and any other form of currency that you brought here with you—into your suitcase or backpack, which will be locked away for safety.

3. You may share certain items. Each of you must identify your own chosen items, but you are free to use someone else's brush or comb, toothpaste, and so on.

4. Exceptions to the above include prescribed medications, glasses or contact lenses, feminine hygiene products, your journal, and a pen. Each participant is encouraged to write journal entries throughout the simulation time to provide a method of processing, questioning, and confession.

5. Those with specific medical conditions, such as sugar diabetes, will be allowed to work out special needs with a facilitator, in order to participate safely. However, participants and their sponsors are responsible for these special situations since facilitators cannot oversee a long list of special needs.

6. All meals cost $6 each. If you eat, you must pay that amount of money—except for the homeless persons, who we will get to in a minute. Meal tickets will be sold ahead of time. You must redeem a ticket in order to receive a meal. You cannot share food with someone else. Only those who purchase meals can eat. The day 2 evening meal is a required meal and everyone must pay for and eat it. The "homeless" persons eat free.

7. Your bed, including room, shower, and utilities, costs $20 a night. If you decide not to pay for rent, you will be able to stay outside in the designated area for sleeping. You are not welcome to come into the building unless invited to do so by a facilitator.

8. One clothing outfit (shirt, pants, and shoes) must be purchased for $3 later today. You may keep any one of your own items that you brought or have on as one of your

four choices, if you wish to do so. You will be asked to change into the one clothing outfit for the remainder of the simulation. Now that we have started, you may not change any clothing.

9. Now regarding homeless people, at least one out of ten of you will not only be poor, but you also will be homeless. You will receive no choice of items and no money. We will provide you with one free exchange of clothes and one meal on Saturday evening. If you eat more than that, it is only because other participants chose to give you some of their money. If you sleep inside, it is only because funds were donated to you. You have no personal sleeping bag, no toothbrush, or any other item, except that which is shared with you by others in the group.

   The homeless among you will be chosen at random, based on numbered tickets drawn from everyone in the simulation. No one is allowed to volunteer to be one of the homeless persons, though each of you may share whatever you wish with those who are picked to be homeless. (Note: With multiple student/adult groups in the simulation, the facilitator may choose to draw one homeless number from each subgroup.)

After reading the rules, give each participant a ticket. The participant is to tear the ticket in half so that the half they keep reflects the same number as the other half they will drop into a can held by a facilitator.

An incredible nervous tension is likely to build as the homeless-person drawing begins.

Carefully pick the first ticket and then purposely read each of the numbers as slowly as possible, to enhance the drama of the choice. As the final number is read, someone will likely scream with anxiety as they recognize the fate of homelessness for the next two days. The others in the room may gasp with thankfulness and then, may feel sadness for the one chosen.

The question of "Why them and not me?" may be the first abstract thought that hopefully will extend throughout the simulation, reminding each one that most of the poor or homeless did not pick their circumstances in life, nor did the wealthy.

Answer a few questions

Up to this point, you purposely should not have answered any of the barrage of impulsive questions from the group. Now it is time to provide a list of answers to frequently asked questions. To control the energized crowd, remind participants that no answer will be repeated, so everyone must listen carefully. You may wish simply to repeat the list here.

EXIT 44

FAQs (Frequently asked questions) and possible leader answers

Question: If we stay outside and it rains, can we come in?
Answer: No, not unless you pay $20.

Question: Can I keep my backpack?
Answer: Everything is an item, including your backpack. You can only keep it as one of your four items.

Question: Do hair scrunches count?
Answer: Everything is an item.

Question: What about my Bible?
Answer: Your Bible is an item. You can only keep it as one of your four items.

Question: I get migraines. Can I keep my medicine?
Answer: If it is prescribed medication, you may keep it.

Question: Where do I put it?
  Answer: That is a middle-class question.
         Figure something out.

Question: What about my retainer?
  Answer: That is a middle-class question.
         (The question should begin to create some irony
         of how differently the poor live from the rich.)

Question: What are we having for breakfast?
  Answer: That is a middle-class question.

Question: Can we share a hairbrush?
  Answer: Yes, you may share any of the four items
         with others.

Question: Is it OK to put on a pair of socks first?
  Answer: Everything you choose from this point on is an
         item. You can have socks, but they are one of your
         items.

Question: What if there are not any shoes that fit?
  Answer: You will be uncomfortable.

Question: Can we change items later?
  Answer: No. You keep all four items throughout the
         simulation time and cannot exchange them.

Question: I am diabetic. Can I keep necessary food?
  Answer: Yes. Your safety is important to us. However,
         remember that the poor might not have that same
         option.

Question: Can I leave early on Saturday evening to go
         to my brother's recital?
  Answer: No. Due to the nature and learning impact
         of the simulation, we ask you to be here for the
         entire time.

Question: What if we do not have money left
for the Saturday night meal?
Answer: It is a required meal and everyone,
except the homeless, must pay.

Question: What if someone hides an extra item?
Answer: Our assumption is that you came here to learn
and are making a commitment to follow these
guidelines. We will not check your pockets
or act as policemen and policewomen for the
simulation. If you cheat, you will ultimately be
the loser.

Question: I just got my ears (eyes, nose, tongue, etc.)
pierced and cannot take it out. What do I do?
Answer: We will cover your exposed jewelry that cannot
be removed with duct tape for the whole
simulation time.

Question: What about my charity or commitment bracelet?
Answer: Same thing.

Question: What if we lose our money or someone steals it?
Answer: You will not receive any extra money.

**The questions may continue for a while, but the leader
must use control to end this time and bring the simulation
to its start. It's time for a prayer of contrition and final
commitment to the Poverty Simulation experience. Say
the following:**

In just a few minutes, we will begin the Poverty Simulation.
What you get out of this experience is based entirely on your
openness and willingness to learn. If you resent being here
and have a negative attitude, you probably will not have a

Plunge2Poverty

great simulation time. However, if you can focus for a few minutes on why you are here—the purpose—and how these few, forsaken privileges that you are giving up can help facilitate a compassionate awareness of the experiences of millions around our world . . . then you can begin to see and care for those whom God cares about and who He wants you to help. Will you pray for that openness and invite God's Spirit to do whatever He needs to do in your life during this simulation time? Will you commit voluntarily to go through this experience and follow these guidelines?

This last commitment of compliance helps participants to own their decision as personal and not forced on them. **The leader or a facilitator may choose to lead in prayer, guide the participants in prayer, or offer a time of silence.**

Let the choices begin

With the prayer ended, remind students that they may get together with others to decide which four items they want to keep for the simulation. A 10- to 15-minute time slot is allowed. Release the group to sort through all of their personal belongings, in order to pick four choices.

This time of selection thrusts the students into an important and often painful time. It also highlights some of the vanity in their lives, especially when participants are forced to think about choosing superficial items, such as lipstick, a hair clip, a cap, or an unnecessary clothing item. It also begins to bond the participants together as they choose to share items and determine what is best for all.

At the end of the allotted time, ask each participant to bring all of their other items to a designated room to be locked up for the rest of the simulation. Remind them that all of their jewelry, money, cell phones, and other personal items should be placed inside their suitcases or backpacks. Ask each participant which four items he or

she chose to keep and then give their money allotment for the simulation.

Two choices must be made immediately after items are put away. Ask participants to decide in the next few minutes whether they plan to eat breakfast the next morning so a meal ticket can be purchased. And they must decide if they are going to spend the night inside and pay the rental fee. A facilitator can collect fees and provide tickets to participants as needed.

Shop 'til ya drop

Based on your local group's unique situation, a location should be prearranged where participants can shop for used clothing. Sometimes a local thrift store will open up for the group, even though it may be as late as 9:30 p.m. before students are ready to visit. Or your local group may collect a wide assortment of very used shirts, pants, and shoes to place in a designated clothes closet or "store" area. **Collect the $3 from each participant for the shopping and only give the group a limited time to make decisions. Remember that they are only paying for shirt, pants, and shoes and can't purchase anything else.**

If they keep any of their own clothing (coats, belts, caps, extra underwear, and so on), these items become part of the four selected items. **Leaders are encouraged not to guide any decision making regarding the clothing.** Even poor choices will become great learning opportunities.

Participants change into those items purchased and then put the extra clothes they were wearing into their suitcase. After everyone is finished, lock that room, closet, or space for the remainder of the simulation.

Bed, bath, or beyond

Bed. Having completed all of the preliminaries, the simulation is now set to provide some great learning opportunities. **Free participants to find their places to sleep and settle**

in for the night. They will awaken tomorrow to a new day of transformation. In most cases, the majority of the group will have opted to sleep outside for this first night. However, since most of them are wired with excitement and the group environment, it may be a long while until they are actually close to sleeping!

The facilitator can monitor the sleeping arrangements to fit the appropriate setting. For example, even though outside and in the presence of adult sponsors, a 1-to-7 ratio is a minimum number of leaders to high school students. **Separate boyfriends and girlfriends.** Since some of the students are sharing sleeping bags, try to allow as much freedom as possible so that their choices are personal and the impact of the long night is based on those choices, not a leader's.

Bath. Acceptable outside bathroom choices are important. **You may want to consider getting portable toilets for the simulation, in order to enhance the challenges.**

Beyond. **A water hose for drinking and rinsing is important.**

Cars. **Participants are not allowed near any vehicles.**

No exit. No one is allowed to leave the designated area under any circumstances.

Lighting, and so forth. **You may consider, based on the local setting and any perceived danger, extra lighting or safety precautions. In addition, inclement weather, such as lightning, subfreezing weather, or hail, can occasionally affect decisions about outside sleeping and cause you to organize a "shelter" on the floor inside the building for a special rate.** (Mission Waco has an overhanging pavilion cover, so we do not bring participants in when it rains. **Remember, the more realistic and difficult the conditions are, the more the impact on these temporary poor.**

Almost without exception, those who sleep outside do not get a good night's sleep. Unusual noises and lights, personal discomfort, and the awkward setting disrupt deep rest. Therefore, most participants will arise already tired before the next long day of the simulation begins. Since the poor often have such interrupted sleep in their noisy neighborhoods, the luxury of comfortable sleep is rare for them as well. This certainly affects anyone's temperament as the day lingers, as our participants will soon discover!

Erratic sleep, occasional food, seemingly unfair demands, physical exhaustion, and loss of the power to control their own schedule will have a multiplier effect on participants' decision making as the simulation progresses. Those participants who may have found themselves blaming the poor for what is often perceived as a self-willed, "lazy" condition will soon discover how days and weeks of physical discomfort, in fact, affect the alertness and clarity of those who are under-resourced.

Soon, it's morning. So let's see what lies ahead!

Second Day Overview:

A Day They Won't Forget

What you will do:

Good Morning, Maybe
Play Time, Sort Of
Lunch, Maybe
Debrief and Process, Absolutely
R&R Time
World Banquet
Debrief and Process
Break
Final Night Session at the Movies

Schedule

7:30 a.m.	Breakfast
8:30–10:30	Training time for Backyard Bible club
10:45–11:45	Backyard Bible Club at a local lower-income site
12:00	Return to training site; start scavenger hunt
4:00 p.m.	Debrief
4:00	Banquet preparation
5:00	Food preparation
6:00–8:00	World Banquet; Chance Cards; ticket sales for bed and breakfast
8:00	Video, followed by group and/or prayertime
10:30	Lights out

Items you will need for the second day and night

- [ ] Cheap soda and stale chips as breakfast food for participants with tickets
- [ ] Game supplies
- [ ] Five-gallon container and lemonade to fill it
- [ ] Paper or plastic cups and paper napkins or towels
- [ ] Cookies or other snacks for the number of people in your Backyard Bible club
- [ ] Copies of appendix 5, page 111: Real-Life Scavenger Hunt; appendix 6, page 115: World Banquet information
- [ ] A garbage bag for cleanup
- [ ] World Banquet volunteer waiters and waitresses in costumes appropriate for the world nations, and items on the shopping list on the following pages (appendix 6)
- [ ] CD player and international music
- [ ] Cards or popsicle sticks color-coded by banquet countries
- [ ] Television with video and DVD player, and videos on poverty (see appendix 8, page 135)
- [ ] Debriefing volunteers
- [ ] Appendix 10, page 149: Chance Cards, and apples

World Banquet shopping list by nation

(*—Denotes item is listed in more than one country or needed elsewhere during the simulation; food quantities must be based on numbers of participants and your Plunge2Poverty budget.)

US

- [ ] Steak
- [ ] Baking potatoes
- [ ] Bacon bits
- [ ] Sour cream
- [ ] Grated cheese*
- [ ] Butter*
- [ ] Rolls*
- [ ] Salad*
- [ ] Salad dressings*
- [ ] Tea*
- [ ] Coffee*
- [ ] Water
- [ ] Ice cream
- [ ] Whipped cream
- [ ] Chocolate topping
- [ ] Vegetable (green)

Europe and Eurasia

- [ ] German sausage
- [ ] Potato salad
- [ ] Coleslaw
- [ ] Rolls*
- [ ] Grape juice
- [ ] Coffee*
- [ ] Apple strudel
- [ ] Water

Latin America

- [ ] Tamales, burritos
- [ ] Canned black beans
- [ ] Corn tortillas
- [ ] Thick coffee*

East Asia

- [ ] Fried rice
      (1 box per 14 people)
- [ ] Hot tea*

Africa/Mideast

☐ Flat bread or tortillas*
(2 per person)

☐ Sweet potatoes

☐ Roasted chicken
(from delicatessen)

South Asia–India

☐ Roasted chicken (deli)

☐ Rice (3 cups raw per
12 people)

☐ Cooking oil for the
curry

☐ Curry

☐ Ginger for the curry

☐ Tomatoes for the curry

☐ Onions for the curry

☐ Cayenne pepper for the
curry

☐ Tortillas*
(2 per person)

☐ Hot tea*

☐ Cardamom for the tea

☐ Cream for the tea

☐ Sugar for the tea

Second Day

A Day They Won't Forget

Good morning, maybe

Some participants have awakened early because, in fact, they could never really sleep. They may wander around to find the other "semicomatose" participants and begin conversations about the difficulty of sleeping in the simulation environment. Possibly they heard dogs barking, trains rattling, nearby snoring, and occasional unidentifiable noises between some winks of rest.

Other people will be seen buried deep in their sleeping bags, hoping for a little more time before their day begins. There are no bells or alarm clocks, so each person eventually will awaken in his or her time. The noise level will grow with the rising sun. A few folks may begin to laugh and even chase each other around.

Everyone is unsure of the next happening and when it will occur, but those who bought a breakfast ticket await some hint of food. Some who did not buy a ticket are now wishing that they had.

In most simulations, student directors find this unplanned morning fun to observe. Most group retreats are planned to the minute; seldom does a group have such a lengthy, spontaneous time together. **In this time block of the early morning, an amazing amount of relationship building and creativity can occur.** Groups may begin to create games out of cups. Others might gather to play a children's game, such as "freeze tag" or "dog pile." Still others could continue to widen their discussion circle about a recent football game, a favorite movie, or other memory. For leaders, it's refreshing to watch youth relate without hand-held games, music and players, and other relationship stoppers.

Call all ticket holders to come to breakfast. As participants zoom to line up, it will take only seconds for them to realize that breakfast is not bacon and eggs or frozen waffles, but stale chips and cheap soda. This is the staple of many inner-city children who stop at the convenience store on the way to school. Somewhere between mad and glad, participants will eat and drink it anyway; at least it is something. But now the distrust of the controlling "middle class," who brought the food, will begin. Participants may wonder, *Should I buy lunch if they are going to give us something like this?*

Playtime, sort of

Around 9:00 a.m., gather all participants for some brief training on how to direct a Backyard Bible Club event. Your group will travel to a nearby housing project filled with excited children waiting for you. **You will need to have a few of your participants to do the following activities and tasks.**

- Prepare to teach a variety of high-action, low-competition games.
- Prepare to teach and perform three or four fun action songs.
- Make a five-gallon cooler of lemonade and arrange a container of cookies or other snack foods.
- Prepare to teach a Bible story with clear lesson goals, including a skit to act out the story and lesson.

You should teach a few rules on handling misbehavior, in case something gets out of hand among the children who will be the recipients of all this planning. Most of all, encourage everyone to serve, participate, and build friendships with the children. Provide any additional guidelines necessary for your group. By 10:00 a.m. relocate your group to the site of a low-income neighborhood or apartment complex.

Check in with the apartment manager or other adult to let him or her know you are on the property and have permission. Ideally, one of your local Poverty Simulation leaders will already know some of the children, parents, and local leaders in this lower-income location where you will conduct the Backyard Bible Club. You may want to connect with other Christian groups who have a presence already in one of the apartment complexes and time your activity so that you assist them with the club.

For the next two hours, your Poverty Simulation participants will interact with lower-income children on their turf. Whether in public housing or Section 8 apartment complexes, many of the middle-class participants present have never been inside such high-density poverty housing. But over the rest of the morning, they will be introduced not only to the possibly rambunctious bunch of children, but also to some of the neighborhood's teens and parents who may wander over to the group.

Let the fun and games begin! **It is the leader's and facilitators' job to help guide the participants through the challenges and show appropriate ways to discipline, encourage, and create a positive environment.** Your Poverty Simulation group will experience and realize how easy it can be to organize and lead a basic Backyard Bible Club. This helps them to realize that they can repeat this same activity in their own community when the Poverty Simulation is over! **Your participants will, with the leader's guidance, help to do the following activities prepared earlier in the day (adjust the scheduled time for each activity to your group's needs).**

- Teach and play a variety of high-action, low-competition games. (15 minutes)
- Perform, teach, and share in three or four fun action songs. (15 minutes)
- Teach a Bible story with clear lesson goals, and participate in a skit that acts out the story and lesson. (15 minutes)
- Serve children drinks of lemonade and cookies or other snack foods, and do cleanup. (15 minutes)

Once ended, it is important to allow your Poverty Simulation group to process the morning's activities. As you walk back to your Poverty Simulation experience site, you will want to have a serious dialogue with participants.

Here are several leader questions you may wish to use.
- How did it feel to be in the apartment complex?
- What did you notice most about the kids? The families? The housing? The environment?
- What positive or negative influences would such an environment have for children and teens living there?
- How did it make you feel to be wealthy (or Anglo) (or from the outside) among them?
- How do you think they felt about you being there?
- What impressed you most about the whole event? (Note: More discussion on processing will follow in the afternoon session.)

Lunch, maybe

When you arrive back at the Poverty Simulation training site, the group may begin to rush to the water hose for drinks or fall onto their sleeping bags to await lunch call. But the next several hours will be filled with a variety of experiences that will stretch participants in new ways. **Long before they are ready, your facilitators should call the group into a huddle for these instructions:**

For the next three and a half hours, you will be on the streets! You will travel only on foot and in small groups of no more than five (youth groups must have one adult sponsor with them, but this person is asked not to organize the group). You must stay with your group. Please do not tell others you meet what you are doing, but seek anonymity so you will be treated without any special favor. Be extra careful and do not take any unnecessary risks. Everyone must be back here by 3:30 in the afternoon without exception (change time as needed to fit your schedule). Since you do not have watches, find other ways to know the time, but do not be late. The address of our location is _____. (Add a few quick landmarks and cross streets for any out-of-town folks to be sure they know how to get back to the site.)

At this point, each group of no more than five persons must organize. Hand out to each group the "Real-Life" Scavenger Hunt sheet (appendix 5, page 111), which lists 17 tasks that each group is to complete before returning back to the site. (You may add or delete certain items for your own context.) Activities include finding a way to eat lunch without real money since they have little or none. Finding a usable item from the dumpster or trash, collecting 100 aluminum cans, and other tasks all have unique purposes, which can be discussed later.

Debrief and process, absolutely

When all the groups have returned, usually exhausted and beaten down from walking the streets, discuss the events of the afternoon. The processing usually takes about an hour. There is journal space on the following pages for leader's to record key participant responses during debriefing.

It is important to have trained volunteer "processors" to help debrief the activity, since this is the first time that real openness to teaching happens. Adult leaders asked to process the event should be reminded:

- The real goal is not only to hear about the experiences, but also to help participants identify their own insights gained from the activities.
- Remind participants of new feelings they had when they connected with the poor or understood something new.
- The processor should avoid frequent attempts to tell his or her insights into such matters, and only model a few personal revelations.

- The processor should go through the "Real-Life" Scavenger Hunt list ahead of time and think of brief insights that might be shared if the right time and opportunity are present.
- The facilitator of the simulation may want to gather these processors together ahead of the simulation and simulate good processing techniques. The debriefing examples shown on this page and the next can be used as a basis for you to write your own debriefing questions.

Each item on the list is read and a person from each street group speaks up to verify whether they completed the activity (if not, why not) and describes some details of the experience. Your goal is to be sure that "connections" happen between their recent street experiences and the ongoing world of the poor. For example, allow each group to share its account of what it was like to find just one meal on the streets. Examples from previous P2P debriefs are shared on the following pages with space for you to record participants' reactions.

Explain many of the reasons, such as mental illness, addiction, and physical disabilities that eventually force people out of homes. Remind participants as needed that some of these men and women are more generous than those of us who have so much.

Take plenty of time for debriefing as you explore the other street tasks participants performed. Ask several groups to read their poem from the Third-World mom whose baby had died in the night. Participants may bow their heads with disbelief that anyone could live through that much pain.

Debriefing examples, and your debriefing record

Leader's journal notes:

_____

_____

_____

_____

_____

_____

_____

Facilitator: Describe your noontime meal.

Answers: "Yeah, we found a dollar and bought bread for lunch."
"We were given five large tacos by a family that couldn't speak English!"
"We didn't eat anything."

Facilitator: "Sounds like it took a lot of energy to find just one meal? How would it be if you had to do that three times a day for yourself and your children?"

Answers: "Man, that would be rough. I don't think I could survive like that!"

Leader's journal notes: _____

_____

_____

_____

_____

_____

_____

Facilitator: What was it like to interact with homeless people?

Answers: "Our Plunge2Poverty group could not find anything to eat, but ran into a homeless man who had the group follow him downtown. Once there, he sold his plasma and then gave us the money to buy food for lunch! Boy, that changes my view of homeless people! My own brother wouldn't do that!"

Leader's journal notes: _____

_____

_____

_____

Facilitator: "What did you find worth keeping from the trash?"

Answers: "We found a good pan."

"We found a working CD player."

"We found some sealed cookies and that's what we had for lunch."

Leader's journal notes: _____

_____

_____

_____

_____

Allow the group to spend a moment processing the way in which people have abused God's resources for our personal greed by telling the short story below, about the Indian family that came to the US.

"An Indian family stayed in our home for a while during a visit to the US. When asked about the biggest impression he had experienced, the man said, 'the size of your garbage cans! It is amazing how much you throw away in this country!'"

When the group is finished debriefing, together say a short prayer of thanksgiving to God for lessons learned on the streets today.

R&R time

From about 4:45–6:00, allow the group to just hang out. For many, this is their opportunity to find a soft place on the ground and snooze a little before the evening meal. Others will enjoy playing, conversing, or writing in their journals. **Again, it is an important time of freedom so that you allow both relationships and awareness of the day's activities to grow.**

During this time, direct volunteers to prepare for the World Banquet. Due to the complexity of cooking six different meals for varying numbers of people, there will be a significant amount of time and preparation done to prepare the banquet food. (You may wish to prepare much of the food, such as steak, baked white and sweet potatoes, coleslaw, potato salad, green salad, roasted chicken (for sanitation, delicatessen chicken may be used), tortillas, burritos, and so forth, in advance. See appendix 6, page 115) for details.)

The volunteer wait staff should begin serving the food with some general instructions to the participants.

For example: You may not share with or receive food from another group. You may not share food with any beggars. You are asked to observe any cultural customs of your continent.

Also provide special instructions such as: "India's participants eat their rice and curry with their right hand only (no forks) because the left hand is considered unclean due to personal hygiene practices; China's participants eat with chopsticks; and so forth."

World banquet and chance cards

By now, everyone is hungry and ready for dinner (no matter what it is!). **Line up participants and invite them into the main dining room that your volunteer staff has prepared. Each participant must draw a card or stick with a color-code or name on it that signifies the dining area they are to sit in for their continent. Volunteer waitresses, adorned in national dress from these global areas, should help participants to find their nation.** Indian, African, Asian, Latin, European, or US music should be playing in the background. Six distinct areas are set to receive their patrons: Africa, Latin America, Europe, India (subcontinent), China (Asia), and the United States (North America).

The numbers of participants eating in each area has been predetermined based on actual global populations (See appendix 6, page 115.) Percentages are according to World Banquet continent. For example: .06 percent of participants for United States dining group). It is important to not allow any changes on who sits where. Only Europe and the United States have chairs to sit in, while all others sit on the floor around some type of tablecloth, plastic mat or map, or slightly decorated section (e.g., a Mexican sombrero might be placed in the middle of Latin America's tablecloth). It quickly becomes obvious that the larger numbers are now crowded for a position, in India and China in particular.

But across the room, the two or three chairs (based on actual numbers of participants in the simulation) that surround the nicely adorned table—complete with white tablecloth, ice-water and wine glasses, extra silverware—soon become the focus of attention. Although each waiter or waitress is attending to their continent's diners, the US waiter or waitress is going overboard to be sure "customers" are taken care of well. For example, he or she may say: "Can I get you cold bottled water, iced tea, or coffee to begin your meal? Or would you prefer all three?" Without much provoking, all other participants begin to realize how these few favored folks will be the focus of the best meal and the most attention.

Each waitress begins to bring out specially prepared meals and drinks for their group.

The beggar.

Soon after everyone is eating, someone portraying a quiet, but filthy beggar should begin to crawl around to various individuals in different continents to seek food. The waiters and waitresses, however, have been told to be sure this "nobody" is ignored and not fed. As the beggar slowly meanders through the crowd with hand extended, most of the participants will try to feed him something. As that happens, the waiter will push him away and take away any food, occasionally saying something like: "You have no right to be here. Leave these nice people alone. Go get a job. You deserve what you get, you worthless beggar!" The remainder of the meal often becomes a serious game between the participants and wait staff to get and to keep him from obtaining food. **To highlight the injustice, for those who attempt to feed him, you may have the remainder of their food thrown into the garbage can. All of this will be debriefed after the meal.**

The wealthy Americans.

As more and more food, including salad, steak, baked potato, green vegetable, extra glasses of iced tea, and so forth, are brought out to the few rich North Americans, the profound unfairness of the nations who experience overconsumption, compared to a world of barely or not enough consumption will sink in. **You may want to even bring in a pet dog and give it the leftover steak to emphasize the waste or preference for our animals over the world's poor.** The crowning moment is when, after almost everyone else is finished eating, a heaping ice-cream sundae with whipped cream and cherry is paraded in front of the others on the way to the Americans' table. The oohs and aahs will fill the room, with occasional "catcalls" that these wealthy folks will be "dealt with later!" It is the perfect atmosphere now for real teaching!

Frustrated feelings and emotions. . . that's good! **Until now, Poverty Simulation leaders, facilitators, and other volunteers have ignored most of the participants' expressed feelings.** The participants are tired, most of them hungry, and many may even have become irritable. Based on their age and maturity, they may begin to say things such as, "This isn't fair!" Such statements now become the basis of the real experiential training.

Facilitators and leaders must remember that emotionless training rarely gets to the inner person's values. But when hunger, sleeplessness, and tiredness are intertwined with feelings of injustice, then the participants begin to feel what most of the world's poor feel every day. **Instead of worrying about "everyone having a good time on this simulation," the leaders and facilitators should now help the group clearly identify those frustrated feelings.**

Debrief and process

At this point in the World Banquet, volunteers need to remove all food, and leaders should ask participants to turn their attention to the leader. He or she will announce:

For the next 45 minutes or so, we are going to process the world in which you ate tonight. We are going to go from continent to continent and ask you some questions about your area. If you do not know the answers for your part of the world, we'll open it up to others, too, from the different nations.

The presentation should continue and include the factual information that follows in this sample:

There are almost 6.4 billion people in your world, most of whom did not choose to be born or live where they are. That was God's choice. You are sitting in a continent with an approximate percentage of persons represented in that part of the world. You can tell by looking that most of the world does not live in the country you come from. In fact, more than half of the world lives in Central (including China) or South Asia (including India). Yet because we have a tendency to become ethnocentric (see ourselves as the center!), many Americans have little awareness or compassion for the rest of the world, especially for the poor.

Today in our world, more than 30,000 children under the age of five died from preventable hunger-related causes. Nearly 1.5 billion of the 6.4 billion people live in what is called *absolute poverty*, meaning they do not have the basic essentials of life (food, clothing, or shelter). Let's learn a few things about each area of the world so we can become better informed and able to make a difference.

At this point, based on background preparation, focus on each continent for about five minutes each. Ask questions such as these, as provided in appendix 6, page 115:

- What did you have to eat?
- What countries are in that continent?
- What are any special customs or cultural mores of that area?
- What is their primary religious worldview?
- How does that particular worldview deal with poverty?
- Are you aware of any special social problems in that area of the world? (See appendix 6 problems, such as hunger, HIV/ AIDS, sexual exploitation of children, and so on.)

Allow each group to try to answer questions about its particular country and then open the discussion to others. The goal is for them to become aware and concerned, so making these points should be personal and passionate, not lecture-style. For example, you can make statements such as:

- If so many children are dying in our world from preventable childhood diseases, why do you think wealthy nations do not help more?
- Or, Europe, which once was a leader in Christian thinking, now has a youth population your age that has abandoned Christianity and calls itself postmodern or post-Christian. Many think the American churches will continue their decline too. Why do you think that is happening? What must change?

Back to us. Once the focus of the debrief finally reaches North America, the group should be ready to get more honest. Though it is a simulation, some now are thinking as outsiders to America for the first time and are more able to be objective after experiencing their meal.

At this point the leader can go several directions with the wrap-up, using various questions such as these:

- The US and Canada make up about 6 percent of the world's population, yet we consume more than one-quarter of the world's resources. Why do you think that is?
- Do you think that our own overconsumption affects others in the world? What do you think Christians should do about that?
- According to most sources, there is enough food in the world for everyone to eat today, yet 30,000 children under age five will die. Do you think Christians in America have a responsibility to do something about that?
- Most churches give less than one-half of 1 percent to the needs of the poor (nationally and globally), yet for the last few decades have spent more and more on their own church needs. What does that say about us?
- What do you think should or could be done about that?
- What personal changes could you make that would help the world's poor?

- Since most of the world's unreached people are poor, what must happen for wealthy American's to reach them?
- Would you consider living incarnate (being the presence of Christ) among the poor to reach them with the good news of Jesus?

Finally, process the feelings toward the beggar and the Americans. We suggest you help the group recognize their tendency is to hide the world's poverty like the wait staff tried to do with the beggar so that we will not be uncomfortable.

- How do we avoid seeing the needs of the poor?
- You heard the wait staff say, "You deserve to be poor." Do Americans sometimes blame the victim for his or her own poverty without offering help?
- How did you who were experiencing other continents feel about the Americans? Help the group learn to widen their feeling-word vocabulary by suggesting words such as *jealous*, *resentful*, *angry*, and others.
- Since we are considered a Christian nation by most of the outside world, can you see how this may affect their view of Christianity?
- How did you who were experiencing American cuisine feel toward the large group out there? Here, you are getting to the key issues. Something such as, "Didn't bother me. That's their problem!" might be said. This obviously opens up a great point of the issue.
- More people will say they felt guilty about having so much while others had so little. Ask: "Do you sometimes feel guilty?"

At this point, affirm that guilt is better than indifference, which is a more common response, but that guilt is not where we want to stay.

- Ask: "How do we move out of guilt into responsibility and joy in giving to others?"

Now the conversation has peaked and the deeper questions are usually being examined.

Each continent's participants are then asked to join hands and pray for their part of the world.

A short emotional break

The World Banquet is physically, emotionally, and spiritually demanding, but begins to get to the key issues of the training. **After the prayer, ask all participants to move outdoors, but on their way, they must take a "Chance Card," similar to one in a Monopoly game (appendix 10, page 149). They must pay (or receive) based on the draw, but everyone is given an apple to satisfy any lingering hunger. During this break, breakfast tickets and any "rent" are collected for anyone wishing to use their welfare money to stay in the beds tonight. While the participants gather to visit and take care of these things, the meeting room is cleaned and a television/DVD is set up. In about ten minutes, invite the group back inside for the final activity of the night.**

Final night session at the movies

The leader should acknowledge participants' tiredness and ask if they are beginning to feel irritable.

Ask: Can you begin to understand how physical and emotional exhaustion can affect your daily attitude and performance? Doesn't poverty have an impact on other areas of your life?

With this introduction, now show a video (see appendix 8, page 135). The chosen video should be well done to hold the group's attention. However, it should be a visual collection of the pain and reality of the world's poor.

Following the video, the leader or some designated facilitator should talk about his or her own journey of change to become more compassionately involved. The group needs to hear of the personal realities of what it takes to change behavior and really sacrifice for the things God calls us to do. Comments about charity, compassion, incarnate living among the poor, overcoming the desire for cultural comforts, and other significant issues are very appropriate.

Then dismiss the group into a brief time of sharing about the day among their peers. Ask participants to conclude in prayer for each other.

After they finish, the structured program of the day is over. Some are ready for bed (even on the hard ground!) and a few others still want to talk a while longer. It has been a long, but powerful day in their lives!

Pulling the Pieces Together for Compassionate Change

What you will do

Breakfast, go to church, lunch, evaluation, clean up, graduation

Schedule

7:00 a.m	Cook and serve waffles, sausages, syrup, and juice
8:00	Worship and sharing time: "What Is God Saying to You?"
9:00	Video
10:00	Leave to walk to church
12:30 p.m.	Prepare and serve lunch
1:00	Give evaluation and posttest; return original pretest and score both
1:40	Clean up building and area
2:30	Group departs

What you will need

☐ Breakfast food

☐ Television and video (see appendix 8, page 135, videos about hunger and poverty)

Pretest/posttest answer key, page 110

☐ A church for worship service

Optional

☐ Graduation T-shirts

Third Day

Pulling the Pieces Together for Compassionate Change

The end is in sight!

It's amazing how much better everyone sleeps the second night of the simulation. Exhausted bodies rest as if they were lifeless with few participants awake early this morning. But as the daylight forces movement, participants eventually are cognizant and remember, *It's over in just a few more hours!* However, a few will recognize the irony of their thought: the real poor have no "end in sight" to their poverty. They will not go home to warm showers, extra food, and too many clean clothes. It's a bitter-sweet thought.

Around 8:30, call for breakfast. This time, instead of inner-city breakfast of soda and chips, it's waffles, sausage, and orange juice! Everyone who bought breakfast is glad now. Within minutes it all will be consumed.

Then call the group into your training area. Since it is the last day, begin this group time with some singing and sharing. There's a soft humility that seems to happen by this time in the simulation. The singing is genuine and expressive. And the sharing time is usually deep and reflective.

The facilitator should ask:

"What has God shown you about yourself during these last few days?" After a few quiet moments, allow participants to answer. Possible answers are:

- "I never realized how selfish I was." "Me, too," says another, "but I am more thankful than I have ever been!"
- "I still wonder how to make changes when I go home."
- "I see my overconsumption now, but I am not sure how to really help the poor and change my habits."

Allow reflections to continue to be expressed. Finally, announce a time of "open prayer" to allow various volunteers to offer short prayers aloud.

With the conclusion of the reflection and singing, it is time to show a second video that will add yet another dimension to the need to follow Christ in His concern for the poor, rejected, and irreligious (see appendix 8, page 135). It should become clear for participants that the Poverty Simulation has not been as much about the poor as it has been about the unwillingness to follow God. The deeper recognition can occur—that ignoring the needs of the poor is a spiritual issue of disobedience and following "other gods."

To prepare to address this issue in the next couple of hours, the leader will want to suggest that participants begin thinking of clear, tangible action steps that each will commit to do after they leave, for the sake of the poor. The key to change must involve solid next steps, and some participants will need to have time to think those through.

Off to church
It is very important that the participants attend a church service where they can experience a different kind of worship with a different cultural or socioeconomic group than they are used to. However, because each Poverty Simulation setting is unique, the choice of where to go to church will vary. Obviously, if you conduct your Poverty Simulation from Friday night until Sunday, you will have many churches to choose from. If you conduct your simulation midweek, be creative in how you arrange for a church service at the appointed time of day. For example, plan a church setting that would resemble a Sunday afternoon service.

In Waco, Church Under the Bridge offers a great blend of people and is currently the primary choice for Poverty Simulations. Before the existence of this church, since the participants were mostly Anglo, they were taken to African American churches (the more vibrant the better!) Usually, we called ahead to be sure we would not be a distraction.

Leader and facilitators should think through what their own group needs to expand their appreciation of other worship styles and expressions. If at all possible, the group should walk to and from church.

Lunch and wrap-up

With church service over, participants will buzz with excitement at the approaching end to the Poverty Simulation. Lunch is the best meal yet. A possible menu is salad, bread, spaghetti or lasagna, water, and ice-cream bars. The purpose of the good meal is to help participants to celebrate God's special gifts of blessings and realize this "unmerited favor."

As soon as lunch is finished, hand each participant three pieces of paper: the evaluation form (appendix 7, page 132), a posttest form (appendix 4, page 106), and then their original pretest. For about 20 minutes, allow everyone to work hard to complete the posttest so that it can be scored. Some participants will need longer than others to work on the evaluation. Quickly grade both pre- and posttests. You should see an obvious improvement in awareness of global realities.

Evaluation

Though participants are usually in a hurry to finish the evaluation so they can begin reclaiming their original belongings, the facilitator should remind them of the importance of this component. Not only do you want participants' insights as to what was most and least meaningful, but it is here that participants make critical decisions about what they can do to take life-changing steps to serve the poor and to follow God's call to bring them "good news."

The next chapter will help to provide them with guidance. The evaluation also helps participants to identify what barriers may sabotage their intentional changes. Be sure you have them write down those barriers since they

are the very issues that can "steal, kill, and destroy" the change process.

The Poverty Simulation certainly confronts the participant with the awareness of the need to change thinking about the poor and usually allows plenty of opportunity to tell someone else about that desired change. However, participants may have only "free-floating" ideas of the various options for change and ill-defined courses of action to commit to change after the simulation ends.

Therefore, it is critical to continue to offer appropriate next steps following the simulation experience and to trust that God will bring about eventual changes in thought and behavior over time, especially with encouragement. Thus, the goal of the leader or facilitator is to find timely ways to affirm the participant, reinforce early changes, and keep processing with him or her on how to keep moving in the action/reflection continuum.

Several factors affect the individual's change process, which itself is unique to each Poverty Simulation participant. An individual's spiritual maturity, which can be self-serving, institutional, internalized, or genuinely "truth seeking" (Peck, 1998), is certainly a factor. Since several of the convictions over the simulation days may directly conflict with parental or cultural values, the change process may feel very costly to the individual. Those who struggle deeply with peer acceptance will find it difficult to reorder certain behaviors (not wearing expensive designer clothing, fasting once a week for the poor, and so on) without internal conflict. The mentor or student director can play a very important role in affirming these counterculture changes.

Each of the four components for change will need reinforcement. Awareness of the needs of the poor must continue past the Poverty Simulation experience. Selected Web sites, magazine subscriptions to Christian groups who work among the poor, prayertimes for the poor, and occasional field trips among the local, national, and global poor are important.

Since human nature fights change, the leader or facilitator who has been told about a participant's desire to change should gently remind the participant of his or her decision and ask how he or she is going to make that decision a reality. One option during this evaluation time is to have each participant write a letter to himself or herself about their personal decisions, then collect those letters and mail them to the participants several weeks following the simulation.

Clean up
Once you open the locked doors to the untouched suitcases and personal items, a kind of chaos breaks out. However, participants can be expected to help sweep, mop, and clean before they leave. Some of them will want to return the "outfit" they have worn since Friday night. **Assign a place for participants to place these clothes.** Volunteers will need to wash and return items as needed. Those who do want to keep their outfits are encouraged to do so since these items become symbols of a life-changing time. Some of the group will continue wearing them for months.

Graduation
Though certainly optional, you can provide a Poverty Simulation T-shirt that symbolizes a participant's graduation from the experience. At Waco, we often sell Poverty Simulation T-shirts after the event to signify participants' unique choice and completion of it. Shirts can be imprinted with: **I saw poverty from the other side!** The (your group's name here) Poverty Simulation Experience. Groups may want to create their own shirt design.

P2P Testimonial

Poverty Simulation Participants' Testimonies

Houston Hendryx, Alpine, Texas

My 21-year-old daughter asked me to participate with her on the Poverty Simulation. It changed my life. As a principal of a middle school, I returned to challenge our teachers to donate clothing to help those who are poor. Thanks!

Bob and Nancy, a married couple from Washington, D.C.

After 17 years of sobriety, my husband and I decided we were ready to have our way of looking at the world changed. We learned about the cruelty and harshness imposed on the poor. We learned what it means to be on the edge. We couldn't wait to leave on Sunday and get back to our normal life, but at the same time we knew we could never be the same. And we aren't. We returned home and knew God was now urging us into action. We have minimized our lifestyle, changed how we use our resources, and turned off the television so we have more time to meet our neighbors. And after several beginning steps, we eventually created a new ministry called God's Stuff, using two large trucks to deliver to those in need the things God has provided through others. My worldview was changed!

P2P Testimonial

Poverty Simulation Leader's Testimony

Dr. Jeff Cook, Cedarville College, Cedarville, Ohio

I use a poverty immersion/homeless experience in a neighboring city at the beginning of my Intro to Urban Ministry course to give students a context for the course. It runs Friday evening to Sunday evening. I have done it three or four times a year for about five years now with about 25 to 30 students at a time (also in January... in Ohio! It's brutal.) They sleep outside regardless of the weather, although in the winter I let them have a fire barrel. I network with several existing ministries in the city. After dressing from the Goodwill, participants are involved with a street evangelism ministry to prostitutes on Friday evening. I introduce them to a former prostitute who shares with them how one ends up on the street. Saturday morning they work with a ministry called Adopt-A-Block, an outreach to the poor in the community where they come face-to-face with people in a strata of society they never knew existed except in movies. Saturday afternoon till evening they just wander the streets collecting cans, digging in dumpsters, and trying to find something to eat. They find out firsthand how demeaning and humiliating it is to ask people for money or food. Late Saturday evening I do an international dinner such as at Waco to focus on global poverty. Sunday morning they visit an urban church, and Sunday afternoon they feed about 200 people at a shelter.

The impact is nothing less than supernatural. On Friday evening they are often terrified... but by Sunday evening they don't want to return to campus. Their eyes have been opened. They have found something that is bigger than they are to invest their lives in. The nearly universal response of students from the simulation is that they are deeply moved, emotional, and often tearful as they say, "This is the most life-changing experience of my life. I never knew this parallel universe existed. I will never be the same." Many believe God now wants them to invest their lives full-time in the city after graduation.

My experience in Waco with you was a great practical help in adding this component to my urban ministry course . . .

My courses are always full, often with a waiting list. It is the buzz of the student body, and those who have gone through the course are the greatest recruiters of other students to take it. Most of our students have been raised in white, upper-middle-class suburbia (it costs about $27,000 a year to go to Cedarville College!), so the urban poor really is a parallel universe . . . but many really want to invest their lives in something other than the context in which they were raised. They want to do something that makes a difference.

What Next?

Change is difficult. One experience is unlikely to bring significant change immediately. Participants who intend to change their behaviors in deference to the needs of the poor need continued reinforcement and support. According to Alan Keith-Lucas in his book Giving and Taking Help, the change process has four components:

1. Awareness of the need to change
2. Telling someone else about that desired change
3. Exploring various options for that change
4. Committing to a course of action

Grasp the Change Process
Explore options

The evaluation time also can offer to participants a brief listing of tangible changes that they can make. For example, the participant may decide to:

1. be a monthly sponsor for a poor child through the World Vision program;
2. trade buying designer clothing for making contributions to the poor;
3. begin serving in a soup kitchen;
4. save a dollar a day for global missions;
5. pray each day for the poor;
6. ask the church finance director how much money the church gives to the local poor;
7. refuse to purchase products from companies that use child labor.

Several participants who attended together may also want to band together to do group projects such as:

1. begin a children's Backyard Bible Club in a local low-income apartment complex;
2. have a monthly day of fasting to remember the poor;
3. decide to not go out for pizza for a few months and donate what they would have spent on a hunger project instead;
4. organize a churchwide hunger-awareness campaign;
5. agree to ask in the next business meeting that the church budget provide increased funding for the needs of the poor.

Now that there is more time to explore these options, the individual or group should agree on a time line to make a decision as to which of the changes or projects considered will be committed into action. Again, it is always important for youth to tell someone else about their decisions, thus deepening the commitment.

Another big option! Since its beginning, Mission Waco (Cross Culture Experiences, Inc.) has been involved with local and global poverty issues. Through 20 years of simulations, participants have been encouraged to find individual or local projects to invest in when they return home from a Poverty Simulation. A tangible, local effort to address poverty will continue to energize a group that has experienced the Poverty Simulation.

However, because the simulation addresses global poverty and increased numbers of Poverty Simulation participants want to be a part of larger projects that help on a national or global level, Mission Waco also encourages participants to consider the following projects and others noted on its Web site, www.missionwaco.org.

1. Haiti Water Well Project—for $2,000, you can provide clean water in a village or area of a village that does not have any by funding the digging of a new water well in northern Haiti.
2. Haiti Orphan Fund—$30 per month will sponsor a child to go to school and get basic care.
3. Mexico City Orphanage—any amount will help support the orphanage for physically and mentally disabled children.
4. Mexico City Urban Ministry Projects—to assist the work of Maranatha Baptist Church with alcoholics, mentally retarded adults, and street children.
5. India Economic Development Project—any amount to support work among outreached people group (Muslim Gujjars) using economic and community development approaches.
6. Mission Waco Benevolence Fund—to help the homeless and poor in Mission Waco's ministry.
7. Church Under the Bridge Special Projects Fund—to help fund activities that assist and reach out to the poor at Church Under the Bridge.

And there are other reputable Christian organizations that you may check out, who are doing significant work among the world's poor:

1. World Vision
2. Compassion International
3. Food for the Hungry
4. Bread for the World
5. International Justice Ministry
6. Woman's Missionary Union
7. The Heifer Project

Keep them accountable

Accountability is critical if the convictions brought by the Holy Spirit during the Poverty Simulation are to translate into values and behavioral changes. The facilitator will want to consider various ways to follow up. For example:

a. Have the student write a letter to himself or herself at the end of the simulation as a reminder of those convictions and intentions gained during the experience.
b. Have the group who attended the simulation to gather once a month to discuss how they are individually or collectively following through with decisions that have a positive impact on the poor.
c. Send an email to each participant with additional facts about global, national, or local poverty.
d. Have a monthly service project for the poor in the local community.

Examine long-term impact

Since the change process is often slow, long-term change may be difficult to gauge. According to studies done on the Poverty Simulation, "the average cognitive increase from 68 percent to 85 percent, a change of 17 percent, is significant. Attitudes towards various cultures, socioeconomic and ethnic groups, are the most impressive. From the posttest discussion questions and the opinion poll (evaluation), it is clear that most students see themselves as more empathetic and sensitive to the needs and choices of the poor" (Dorrell, 1993).

But real change must exhibit itself in ongoing action that addresses the needs of the poor and marginalized. Habits of prayer for the poor, personal financial sacrifice to provide assistance to their needs, adoption of projects that deal with systemic poverty, trips to Third-World countries, and other efforts are consistent with genuine change.

Perhaps the most powerful witness of the Poverty Simulation's impact has been the testimonies of scores of participants who went through the training over the past 20 years. They have written to say that this particular experience was a catalyst to their decision to work among the poor as teachers, missionaries, hunger and community development organizational workers, and urban ministers, as recounted in the testimonials in this guidebook.

Poverty simulation modifications and options

Every training context is unique and the exact design presented here will not always fit each group's special needs. However, the basic model can be easily adjusted to fit your circumstances.

What do you want to accomplish?

Forethought and preparation are the keys to any good training event. We encourage leaders to think through the outcomes desired before making a commitment to the simulation. Because real change will involve more than merely attending the Plunge2Poverty Simulation experience and should require some ongoing awareness, accountability, and motivation, the more you as a leader prepare ahead of time, the greater the impact on students. Leaders also may want the support of their church or pastoral staff and team on this journey.

Questions you may want to consider include:

1. By taking my group through a Poverty Simulation, I hope and pray that they will...
2. If we had a great experience and several of the group wanted to make some real changes in their lives, I would suggest that they...
3. Some of the challenges I can anticipate on a stretching experience like this are...
4. Because I realize the impact such a time has varies with individual spiritual maturity, I may want to ____ before and after the training.
5. Are there any students that should not be allowed to attend and why?
6. If only a few of the students are highly affected and desire to make changes, is it worth it to conduct this Poverty Simulation?
7. If your group consists primarily of high school students: How should I prepare the parents before the experience

and how do I process it with parents after the training, knowing there will be a variety of implications about values surrounding wealth and poverty?

Your training setting

The ideal community: Since training about poverty is your goal, the ideal setting for your Plunge2Poverty Intensive Poverty Simulation Experience is a local lower-income area in or near your community. Though they may rarely think of making a difference right in their own city, the more your group members plunge into a deprived or blighted neighborhood in their community, the greater the awareness of local need.

Obviously, a safe setting with reasonable risk is important to assure parents, participants, and organizational leaders that no harm will come to the participants. (Note: Mission Waco's context is a low-income area of the city with significant cultural and ethnic diversity and nearby housing complexes. Mission Waco has been leading the Poverty Simulation for more than 20 years and has never had an incident related to the training site.)

If your group is located in more of a middle-class neighborhood or area of the city, consider a partnership with a local nonprofit that works among the poor and try to use its building for your simulation. Or perhaps you can locate a church in a poorer area that would rent their facilities to you for a weekend or the several days of your simulation. You also could join the church for Sunday worship if its congregational blend fits the earlier description suggested.

If high school students make up part of your training group, consider having a parent's meeting at the site a few weeks before the simulation, and have those involved in that neighborhood assure all concerned of the safety precautions being taken. You also may want to notify local police or security personnel of the upcoming event and ask for additional attention to the area you will use.

Occasionally, due to exaggerated fear, there will be some parents who will decide not to allow their high school student to attend. Affirm their concern for their student, but we suggest that you continue your event, even if the numbers dwindle. We have found that, after the first successful event, the excitement of those who completed it will still be significant and parents who resisted will allow their students to come the next time you offer the simulation.

The ideal building

You will want to have a room large enough for group discussions and the World Banquet, a kitchen, and an enclosed backyard area for those who choose to sleep outside. Since walking distance to the Backyard Bible Club site and the Sunday (or other day of the week) morning worship site is important, try to find a building that is reasonably close. If your building and site work well, but you must transport participants to and from these activities, this may still work well for your group.

Some groups will have a more unique intention in their training goals. For example, if homelessness is the focus, you may want to consider working with a local shelter to provide accommodations for your group to sleep in the shelter. Particularly, if they are college students or adults, you also may want to have them on the street for longer periods of time and meet occasionally for content and processing at different sites throughout the simulation.

Though a middle-class setting is discouraged (if that is the only option), the simulation still can provide significant impact if other components are included. For example, participants could be shuttled to lower-income neighborhoods and urban ministry sites for involvement there.

Participants

• **Students and families.** Due to the importance of working with participants who are capable of abstract thinking, Mission Waco determined after a few years of allowing middle-school students to attend, that the goals of its Poverty Simulation could not be adequately accomplished with that age group.

There was never a question of middle-school students' resilience or their ability to endure the challenges of the simulation. However, their ability to connect the experience with personal reflection and make the changes necessary to affect the poor was minimal. Therefore, Mission Waco allows students who have completed the eighth grade and those who are in high school to attend the Poverty Simulation. Exceptions are made.

Families who want to attend together with their younger children may do so. In the case of our youth groups, Mission Waco requires a 1/7 adult-to-youth ratio, and the parents of the younger students must participate in the simulation with their youth. (Note: Though adults should participate with students, they should not control the learning event. Allow youth to lead out in the various small- and large-group settings as much as possible.)

Some groups do want to include and focus on middle-school-age participants. In these cases, it is best that this age group be the only group involved and use a much tighter and more supervised schedule. Participant numbers should be lowered. The outcomes will need to be more directed as well.

• **College students and adults.** Older participants seem to learn and process significantly more during the same simulation event. Since Mission Waco's training is open to a maximum of 75 students per training event, various groups from different locations may schedule the simulation. The mix of various older groups has not seemed to impede the learning process.

However, we also have found that college students are generally negatively affected by the younger high-school-age students, whose learning styles and maturity level may be generally less developed and can distract the others. Therefore, you may want to consider just offering the Poverty Simulation only to high school or college/adult groups rather than combining the two groups.

• **Leadership age.** The minister of youth's age and spiritual maturity has also been a significant factor in the outcomes for his or her group. A student leader who is not fully supportive of the simulation activities can have a negative effect on the growing intensity of the youths' emotions during their experience. Again, we suggest, if at all possible, the minister of youth should attend a Poverty Simulation prior to bringing the youth group.

The schedule

The power and impact of the Plunge2Poverty experience cannot be reduced to one or two events, but comes from a combination of many of them. There is something unique in the cumulative effects of the individual components. Throughout the years, the Poverty Simulation evaluations indicated a wide variation in which portions of the scheduled activities were more transformational for the participants.

The proposed schedule can be necessarily modified and still have significant impact to train students about poverty. However, since the included schedule has been successfully adjusted during 20 years of positive implementation, student directors are encouraged to make any schedule changes with careful consideration, especially since there may be unintended accompanying loss of impact with these changes.

For example, though the World Banquet can be a powerful stand-alone activity for a church or missions banquet, its real power comes when students have had nothing or little for breakfast, have been on the streets for hours to find a meal, and then end up in India that evening, eating rice and curry (with their hands!) without any recourse for food later in the night. The emotional effect, compounded by the lack of food for a full day is significant! Having the banquet as the last event of the day, then going home to eat from a full refrigerator of food lessens the intensity of the simulation.

Interaction time with the poor or marginalized

While playing with lower-income children is one of the easiest ways for students to overcome their fear of people who may seem intimidating or different to them, other interactions may be substituted. If for any reason your group cannot arrange an appropriate Backyard Bible club site, you may consider encounters with other lower-income persons or marginalized groups. The homeless, mentally ill, imprisoned, those in a detention center, children with special needs, the addicted and other groups, which are likely new encounters for your participants, will be best. While nursing homes are not unimportant, many of the participants have visited there before. If you do choose a nursing home, consider a county- or state-run facility that accepts mostly patients with no money or government subsidy.

Ideally, your experience should be relational and sustained for at least an hour and a half. It certainly should not be a casual observation, but one in which interaction with the poor and needy helps your participants realize the humanity of those with whom you are working.

Activities
The "Real-Life" Scavenger Hunt

Some activities on the "Real-Life" Scavenger Hunt can be changed to accommodate the needs and resources of your group. While almost all of the list included in the appendix can be done in most places, there may be wisdom in adjusting the list so that it can enhance your group's experience. Because time limitations will affect the modified schedule, be sure to have realistic expectations about how much can happen in the allotted time slot.

It is still important to maintain as much anonymity as possible for the participants so that they will not be treated with any special favors. If your group feels as if they have been deceitful by remaining silent about their identities, assure them that they can return after its conclusion to explain more of what occurred.

Intensity. The most important scheduling portion of the entire Poverty Simulation is its intensity, which directly relates to its longevity. Experiential educators know that peak experiences that are sustained over longer periods of time have a higher change influence on the participants than shorter experiences. In the Poverty Simulation, the two-night experience has a significantly higher impact than a single-night training event. In fact, it is usually the second evening and following morning when many of the real breakthroughs occur for most participants. The ability to intrinsically understand the impact of poverty from the numerous demands and frustrations of the simulated life usually causes them to say, "Now I understand!"

Four- and five-day summer simulations. In the earliest days of the summer program, we even had groups continue it for four or five days! The experience over so many days led to an even more vivid understanding of the life of the poor, and the emotions of sustained days ran high. Many of those students who went through the simulation more than 15 years ago continue to talk about the week as the catalyst that changed their lives. Though the weekend or two day/one night itinerary is a shorter Poverty Simulation, we have found that the learning curve during that time is still strong.

If your group simply cannot do as much as a two-night simulation, it is important to lessen your expectations and also work harder at condensing the available schedule with as much training as possible. For example:

• Begin as early in the morning as you can.
• Continue until it is late.
• Create additional guidelines, such as not eating after they return home.
• Meet at a low-income, ethnic church the next day, and so forth.

Since each component has its own influence on what different individuals learn, the facilitator will have to choose carefully what to exclude.

Changing to a weekday setting, particularly in the summer

months, may be considered if the weekends will not work for you. Remember, your worship experience is important in building a deeper connection with different members of the Christian community, so you will have to consider other settings and groups you can worship with on the weeknight experience rather than Sunday morning. Wednesday evening, Friday night, or Saturday night services and other settings may be available in your area.

Special training emphasis. Some groups have used the Plunge2Poverty experience as a precursor for their own missions trip to a lower-income country. At least one group completed the weekend and left immediately from the Poverty Simulation to a Third-World site. Other groups have used the weekend for staff training for their nonprofit organization involved in providing assistance to the poor.

In these cases, modifications can be made to highlight the unique setting. For example, language learning, cultural sensitivity, and team-building activities can be inserted. In a longer simulation, one group added certain Third-World building techniques. Another group tacked on a full "ropes-challenge course" training experience to build more trust and communication.

Some unique settings have even lend themselves to taking some of the ideas into basic orientation in other countries. For example, the "Real-Life" Scavenger Hunt was adapted for the first few days for a group missions trip to New Delhi, India. Group members had to do a number of activities, including find locations via city buses, learn certain words in Hindi, eat cultural foods, exchange money, and so on.

Feel free to be creative with this simulation and create an experience suitable to your group's needs.

The minister of youth's age and spiritual maturity has also been a significant factor in the outcomes for his or her group. A student leader who is not fully supportive of the simulation activities can have a negative effect on the growing intensity of the youths' emotions during their experience. Again, we suggest, if at all possible, the minister of youth should attend a Poverty Simulation prior to bringing the youth group.

Do's and don'ts for effective experiential education

Experiential education is nothing new. In fact, most training throughout history occurred as skilled artisans and craftsmen took an apprentice under their wings to show them how to master the various tasks. Unfortunately, cognitive-based education became the primary model of education in the Western culture. Unlike the biblical understanding of "knowing" based on doing, most education today is merely a regurgitation of facts and figures. After centuries of sitting in stoic classrooms, many US secondary and university students today have become adept with information (theory) but weak in practical skills (practice).

Various educational models, such as John Dewey's approach, the Montessori Method, and a rise in "Service Learning" on many campuses, have attempted to correct the glut of information with more balanced learning through the integration of both theory and practice. Yet churches tend still to rely on the assumption that Bible studies, sermons, and Sunday School classes will have a strong impact on behavior. Research suggests, however, that much of this information has little effect on confronting the values of the world. Christian youth, for example, cheat on tests, become involved in premarital sex, and value materialism as much as their unchurched peers.

How students learn has been debated for centuries, but almost all educators agree that there are different models that accelerate internalization of information that is unique to the individual. Some students prefer a more visual approach, some auditory (listening and speaking), and others kinesthetic (movement and touch), though all are used in some way. Good teachers will use a variety and combination of the different styles to reach their students.

In 1975, David A. Kolb and Roger Fry created their own learning theory around four elements: (1) concrete experience,

(2) observation and reflection, (3) the formation of abstract concepts, and (4) testing in new situations. These operate in a learning style that builds on each component part. These ideas have been tested and developed by several educators. And while everyone does not agree with their conclusions, most classroom teachers will at least admit that a variety of styles of teaching enhances learning in any classroom.

In other words, an experience such as the Poverty Simulation becomes the concrete experience that causes participants to reflect on the various components of being poor, and then form new ideas about the issue. Instead of dry lectures, which quote statistics and conditions of poverty, the participant actually feels and experiences aspects of poverty. Students who are developing and growing abstract-thinking skills can be led through a reflective process around those experiences in order to develop new ideas and overcome other thoughts. For example, a participant who comes to the simulation experience thinking that "poor people are lazy," feels exhaustion and weakness with little food, receives limited sleep, and walks several miles on the streets. Then that student can reorder his or her misconceptions by admitting that the physical demands on the poor can diminish their entrepreneurial spirit and their ability to overcome poverty by sheer willpower or action.

Creating meaningful experiences. Student workers and Christian educators will recognize quickly how enthusiastic their youth group becomes when the students leave the church building to paint a house for a poor person, go on a missions trip, or do a fund-raising activity. Activity tends to energize many who struggle to sit still in a classroom setting.

However, while activities are beneficial, their real impact comes when the teacher/facilitator uses the experience as a point of reflection.

P2P Testimonial

Poverty Simulation Participant's Testimony

Kristen Titcombe, Minneapolis, Minnesota

We were amazed by the kindness and generosity of the people experiencing homelessness that we met. Confronted with new situations, we weren't sure who to trust. Women, men, and couples all went out of their way to tell how we could find clothing, food, shelter, and support groups. They offered us rides, and resource guides. People who helped us told us where we could get a job, or an identification card. Everyone who helped us was currently homeless, or had been at one point, and they shared with us whatever they had. Other more financially secure people ignored us, treated us suspiciously, or looked at us as if we were subhuman.

We heard firsthand stories of people who had come to the cities alone for a job and lost their housing, men who had fought in Vietnam, and young women who had traded sex daily for a place to sleep. And our hearts broke.

We talked as a group about the call to "loose the chains of injustice and untie the cords of the yoke, to set the oppressed free and break every yoke. Share your food with the hungry and to provide the poor wanderer with shelter—when you see the naked, to clothe him, and not to turn away from your own flesh and blood."

The call seems so clear. We are charged to set the oppressed free, and to share our food, clothes, and housing with those who are in need. But we struggle to know how to help people in an unsafe world. We want to help our own flesh and blood who are camping in the woods, or staying at one of the cities' shelters.

P2P Testimonial

Poverty Simulation Participant's Testimony

Megan Handley, Indiana

I just graduated from Bible school and am pursuing full-time ministry, either in the inner city here in the States or overseas. I also have the desire to mobilize young Christians for the missions field, and hope that wherever I end up, I will be able to encourage and challenge younger believers. I found that the Poverty Simulation was a helpful resource for me. I'm not sure exactly how and when it will be used, but as I continue to prepare myself for whatever God has for me, I want to learn from the knowledge and experience of other, wiser people. I will also be lending it to the youth pastor of my home church in Indiana. He will be bringing up the youth for a missions trip to Chicago this summer, and is planning to do a scavenger hunt similar to the one found in the Poverty Simulation. Thank you for your help and the work that you do.

P2P Testimonial

Poverty Simulation Leader's Testimony

Mary Morrison, Founder of God's Stuff, Washington, D.C.

During the Poverty Simulation, the group at Mission Waco carefully allowed us to learn and safely experience more about international poverty in Third-World countries, poverty in our communities, and what it means to live on the edge of poverty every day. We also learned about the harshness and cruelty of the world that is imposed on these people daily. I was particularly enlightened in my understanding of the trials of the homeless. Honestly, I couldn't wait to leave on Sunday and go back to my normal life, but at the same time all of us confirmed on our way home that we would never be the same. This experience changed how we looked at the world and life would never be the same again. Janet's words stuck with me and I kept thinking, "What can I do?"

We started out not knowing what to do and God's Stuff continues to grow and expand. I now have so many things that I've become interested in doing that I don't have time to do them all. The Poverty Simulation experience changed the way I view the world. I have minimized my lifestyle. I don't hold onto things I don't use or need when I know so many need so much. It even helped me, along with prayer, to change how I use my resources; my time and my money. It's no longer important if I see that television program or have time to read the newspaper every day; it's really wonderful to meet so many of our neighbors. Their thanks and hugs and tears make it all worthwhile and the God moments we have experienced make me understand the meaning of "awesome." The best part is that I know my journey has only started!

PLUNGE2POVERTY
APPENDIXES

Poverty
Simulation Tools

Poverty Simulation Sample Schedule

First Night

8:00 P.M.	Welcome!
	Complete/collect release forms
	Collect any fees
	Give pretest;
	Explain rules of the simulation
	Answer a few questions
	Draw tickets for "homeless" persons
	Remind participants that experiencing the Poverty Simulation is by voluntary choice, but that they must remain if they have decided to participate.
8:45	Breakout time to choose items and put away "extras."
	Purchase of breakfast cards and inside privileges for those who choose.
9:00	"Thrift store" shopping to get secondhand clothing for simulation, and packing of belongings
11:30	Lights out

Second Day

7:30 A.M.	Breakfast of chips and cheap soda
8:30–10:30	Training time: games, stories, leadership skills for Backyard Bible club
10:45–11:45	Backyard Bible club; visit a local lower-income apartment complex
12:00	Return to training site; send out on scavenger hunt
4:00 P.M.	Debrief—One facilitator to process experience for each 12 to 18 participants
4:00	Start banquet preparation with other volunteers

5:00	Food preparation begins; 8 to 9 servers plus "beggar"
6:00–8:00	World Banquet, followed by Chance Cards and apples; sell tickets for breakfast and sleeping in
8:00	Video, followed by group and/or prayertime
10:30	Lights out

Third Day

7:00 A.M	Cook and serve waffles, sausages, syrup, and juice
8:00	Worship and sharing time: "What Is God Saying to You?"
9:00	Video
10:00	Leave to walk to church
12:30 P.M.	Prepare and serve lunch
1:00	Give evaluation and posttest; return original pretest and score both to determine amount of cognitive change
1:40	Clean up building and area
2:30	Group departs

Information to Churches and Parents Sending Participants

Dear Youth Pastor/Parent,

The Scriptures are clear: God cares for the poor and marginalized and has called us to be involved with them—to bring them the good news of Jesus Christ. Unfortunately, much of our discipleship has ignored this important command.

This unique simulation, Plunge2Poverty, is designed to help train participants about the realities of our world of need, God's heart for the poor, and how we can better live out God's call for us to connect with the poor. For more than 20 years, groups have been "experiencing" poverty through this intensive Poverty Simulation experience.

To date, no one has ever been hurt during this experience. But the simulation will stretch participants outside their "comfort zones" to face their own materialism, cultural values, and need to refocus on the biblical mandates.

Because too much information takes away from the impact of the simulation, there are many details that we do not give out. However, if you or some adult involved really wants more information than what is provided below, just give us a call (but please do not tell the participants!).

And we hope they return home with "new eyes and ears" for the needs of the poor in your own community, our nation, and the world. Thanks for encouraging this important development for them. Please pray that God will do great things in their lives during Plunge2Poverty!

Here are some FAQs (frequently asked questions):

What do we bring? You will pack as if you were going on a simple retreat. A sleeping bag, pillow, extra clothing, and so on, is encouraged. We discourage bringing jewelry, lots of money, and electronic games and CD players.

Is the simulation safe? You will never be alone. You will **always** be supervised. You will be safer in this simulation experience than you might be at your local mall.

What should I expect? To glimpse things about yourself that you did not know and would not necessarily choose to know.

Will I be miserable? You will need to pack a good attitude and have a desire to know your Lord and Redeemer in a deeper way. When you love someone, you know what breaks their heart.

What will I eat and where will I sleep? You will have some choice of necessities, such as food and shelter.

What ages can participate? You must be 14 years of age or older. You will need to have completed the eighth grade.

Why don't you allow junior high students? The simulation requires thought processes and focused conversations that often bore someone younger than 14 years old. Attention spans need to be longer. We do have other things in our ministry for junior high students to do, such as work projects, interactions with low-income children, and street camps!

What if someone has a special diet or needs medication? No problem! This person will need to bring items for the special diet and their medications. Personal health is important to us.

What if some of the group cannot come for the entire simulation? Then they should come at another time when they can stay for the entire simulation. The impact is considerably lessened if they leave. The simulation **starts at 8:00 P.M. sharp** on night one and ends on day three at 2:00 P.M. Only 42 hours long (or your program schedule)!

Appendix 3

Release Form

(Sample Only)

Note: Have your own legal representative review for additional suggestions.

Release of Liability and Parent Permission Form
(For youth under age 18)
Cross Culture Experiences, Inc. (dba Mission Waco)

**Required for the following activities
(check all that apply for this release):**

☐ Poverty Simulation, Waco, Texas,
    628 N. 15th, Waco, TX

☐ Climbing Wall at Jubilee Center,
    1319 N. 15th, Waco, TX

☐ Out of Country Mission/Exposure Trip:
    Specify which country _____

☐ Special Outing or Field Trip:
    Describe _____

☐ Mission Waco Program(s) including transportation:
    Describe _____

☐ Volunteerism in Mission Waco Programs

☐ Construction/Work Projects

Whereas, the undersigned participant wishes to be accepted for participation in one or more of the activities listed above, which is organized by Cross Culture Experiences, Inc. / Mission Waco, of Waco, Texas, and regarding Cross Culture Experiences, Inc. / Mission Waco's action in allowing the applicant to participate in such activities or programs, the undersigned acknowledges that the activity does involve certain risks. The activities are designed to allow the participant to broaden their understanding of various Christian values, socioeconomic differences, ethnic and racial diversity, cultural appreciation, team building, character development, and/ or enrichment opportunities. These activities include those listed above, but are not limited to, and activities in a lower- income neighborhood and among poor people in Waco, Texas, other communities, and foreign countries.

I understand that participants are exposed to physical and psychological risk through elements of nature, travel by car, van, plane, walking, or other conveyance, and direct contact with people from various backgrounds. Risks may also include damage or loss of personal property. I further understand that immediate medical treatment may be difficult or delayed, especially in foreign countries. Risks may also include physical injury and/or strenuous physical activity at work/construction sites, the Climbing Wall, or during other activities.

In consideration of the above, I have and do hereby assume all the above risks and any other ordinary risk incidental to the nature of the program, including risks which are not specifically foreseeable, and will hold harmless and indemnify Cross Culture Experiences, Inc. / Mission Waco, its Board of Directors, employees, agents, and/or associates from any and all liability. The terms hereof, and my signature on this document shall serve as a release and assumption of risk, and shall bind my heirs, representatives, executors, administrators, successors and assigns and for all members of my family, including any minors accompanying me. I also state that I am not under, and will not be under the influence of any nonprescribed chemical substance, including alcohol. I also state that I will assume responsibility for any damage or loss to physical property or expenses incurred due to negligent or irresponsible behavior. I understand that my participation in this Cross Culture Experiences / Mission Waco Program or activity is entirely voluntary.

My signature also gives my permission and accepts financial responsibility, as well, for first-aid treatment and/or professional medical attention if needed. I also give permission for photographing of myself or my child during the activities and use of those pictures or video by Cross Culture Experiences, Inc. / Mission Waco.

_____   _____
Participant Signature   Date

_____   _____
Witness   Date

_____   _____
Parent/Guardian Signature   Date

_____   _____
Witness   Date
(For any participant under age 18)

Please print legibly. Each participant must complete this section:

Participant Name: _____

Age:_____Phone: (___)_____

Address: _____

City/State: _____ZIP:_____ .

In case of emergency, please contact: _____

Phone: (   ) _____

Contact's relationship to participant: _____

Pretest/Posttest

Each question is worth 2 points: subtract from 100.

Name:_____ **Age:** _____

Date: _____   **Final Grade:** _____

Match the following with the most appropriate words:

1. Shalom	A. Muslims
2. TANF	B. Number of people per square mile of India
3. Hinduism	C. A branch of Christianity
4. 722	D. Living among the people with whom you work
5. Holistic	E. Karma
6. Incarnation	F. Cultural emphasis on possessions
7. Stewardship	G. Welfare to Work Program
8. Orthodox	H. Old Testament idea similar to kingdom of God
9. Materialism	I. All belongs to God: I use what I have for Him
10. Islam	J. Ministries which include mental, physical, and spiritual aspects

Circle the best answer for each of the following:

11. What percent of the world's population now live in sizeable cities?

    a. 10 percent   b. 25 percent

    c. 50 percent   d. 75 percent

12. What percent of the world's population is Anglo?

    a. under one-fourth   b. one-third

    c. one-half   d. three-fourths

13. The country with the second largest population of Muslims is:

    a. India   b. Haiti

    c. Pakistan   d. Turkey

14. The world's population is approximately:
    a. 912 million   b. 6.5 billion
    c. 100 billion   d. 1 trillion

15. The phrase "foreign missions has come home" means:
    a. Most missionaries have been expelled from the
       country in which they work.
    b. Finances are forcing missionaries to come back to the
       States.
    c. Large groups of people from other faiths are now
       living among us in the US.

16. According to the US Federal Poverty Guidelines, a
    family of four must make under:
    a. $25,000/year   b. $18,850/year
    c. $10,400/year   d. one million/year

17. Approximately how many children under age five die
    daily from hunger-related causes?
    a. 350   b. 3,100
    c. 30,000   d. 1 million

18. There are approximately how many persons in the world
    labeled as the "absolute poor"?
    a. 3,100   b. 31,000
    c. 1.4 million   d. 1.4 billion

19. One of the main reasons churches do not care about
    people's human needs is:
    a. Decreases in giving.
    b. "Greek dualism" theology divides souls from daily
       lives.
    c. Churches are not called to the poor.
    d. Poor people take advantage of the "system."

20. Which of the following is not considered a religious cult?
    a. Jehovah Witnesses b. Mormons
    c. Nation of Islam   d. Catholicism

Rank order by putting a 1, 2, or 3 by each of the following:

21. The largest religion in the world:
    _____ Islam   _____ Christianity   _____ Hinduism

22. The largest population in the world:
    _____ New York City _____ Tokyo _____ Mexico City

23. The poorest country in the world:
    _____ Chad, Africa _____ Haiti _____ India

24. The largest church membership in the world:
    _____ Seoul, Korea _____ Dallas _____ Paris

25. List two Scriptures from the Bible that talk about God's concern for the poor:
    a.

    b.

26. For each of the following cities, list the country and primary religion:

City	Country	Primary Religion
Jakarta		
São Paulo		
Cairo		
Calcutta		
Bangkok		
Addis Ababa		

Sources: www.census.gov, www.ibiblio

True/False

_____ 27. The greatest barriers to effective ministry in the cities are in the churches.

_____ 28. Because poor people have limited skills and resources, it is best to begin ministries for them instead of with them.

_____ 29. Most "hard-living people" (e.g., alcoholic, several divorces, drug abuser, homeless, etc.) have a strong disrespect for God, but respect the church leaders.

_____ 30. Most people read the Bible through "rural lenses."

_____ 31. All Christians are called by God to help the poor and oppressed.

_____ 32. More than 50 percent of Christian missionary church planters are working with the fastest growing world religion.

_____ 33. The greatest migration in human history is happening now as people move to the cities.

_____ 34. Racial issues are no longer a problem in the US judicial system.

_____ 35. The rich are still getting richer, while the poor are getting poorer.

_____ 36. Just as there is a personal sin, there is also "corporate" or "systemic" sin.

1.	H	13.	A
2.	G	14.	B
3.	E	15.	C
4.	B	16.	B
5.	J	17.	C
6.	D	18.	D
7.	I	19.	B
8.	C	20.	D
9.	F	21.	2 1 3
10.	A	22.	3 2 1
11.	C	23.	1 2 3
12.	A	24.	1 2 3

25. Isaiah 58; Matthew 25, Matthew 6
26. Jakarta,Indonesia, Islam
    Sao Paulo, Brazil,Catholic
    Cairo, Egypt, Islam
    Kolkata, India, Hindu
    Bangkok, Thailand, Buddhist
    Addis Ababa, Ethiopia, Orthodox

27.	T	32.	F
28.	F	33.	T
29.	F	34.	F
30.	T	35.	T
31.	T	36.	T

Appendix 5
"Real-Life" Scavenger Hunt

During the next several hours, you will be "on the streets." Although most of the poor would not be in small groups and have certain "built-in" middle-class resources, as you will, the following tasks are designed to give you a better understanding of the harsh realities of those who are poor.

To get the most out of the afternoon, please follow these guidelines:

- Do not explain to those you meet that you are in a Poverty Simulation. Do not be deceitful, but do try to avoid volunteering that information.
- Record your activities as much as possible.
- Stay in your group. Some tasks may be done by just one person in your group, but groups are not to separate.
- Vehicles are off-limits. Do not get in anyone's car.
- Be careful. Avoid any situation that seems too risky. Don't take foolish chances that will jeopardize your safety. Call the (your church) office phone number here:_____ or cell here: _____ if there is a problem.
- Do all of the activities. There is enough time if you will pace yourself.
- Be back at 4:00 P.M. to the church at [address]: **Do not be late!**

Checklist of Activities

- [ ] Eat lunch. (Yes, this is your only noon meal.)
- [ ] Interview a homeless person. (Please treat this person with respect!)
- [ ] Borrow a quarter from someone you do not know. (Note: Asking for money on the street corner or in a local business is against local ordinances.)
- [ ] Retrieve a useable item from a dumpster.
- [ ] Collect 100 aluminum cans and find out the current rate of redemption.

☐ Record a negative "sense experience" for each of the following:
- Touch _____
- Sound _____
- Taste _____
- Sight _____
- Smell _____

☐ Write a letter to an unknown prisoner.

☐ Write a poem from the viewpoint of a Third-World mother whose child died in the night from hunger.

☐ Visit with an elderly person.

☐ One person in the group should give something away to someone outside the group.

☐ Ask someone who goes to church how much money they think the average Christian gives to the needs of the poor in [your city or town]. $ _____ / year.

☐ Write out a budget for a poor family of four (one adult, three children) for a month:

Income:

Minimum wage working 30 hours a week:
$_____/month

Expenses:

Rent:	$_____
Utilities: (electricity, gas, water)	$_____
Food:	$_____
Transportation:	$_____
Clothing:	$_____
School costs:	$_____
Medical:	$_____
Recreation:	$_____
Total expenses:	$_____

Difference between income (+) and expenses (−) per month:
$_____

13. Write down the average value of all the participants' personal possessions that are locked in the closet (total everyone's amount and divide by number of members In group). Include estimated cost of furniture, clothes, shoes, electronic devices, jewelry, and other items $___ _____ per person

14. Ask someone where the poor go to get help with the following:
    Emergency shelter:
    Food assistance:
    Rent or utility assistance:
    Transportation assistance:
    Medical assistance/medicine:
    Alcohol/drug recovery:

15. Find out what area of town most of the following groups live in:
    The wealthy:
    African Americans:
    Hispanics:

16. Find out what each of the following is:
    Section 8 housing:
    WIC:
    Parole:
    Twelve-Step program:
    SSI.:
    Schizophrenia:
    Sclerosis of the liver:

17. Read Matthew 25:31–46 and identify the following:
    Who are the "sheep"?
    Who are the "goats"?
    Who are "the least of these"?
    What is the "inheritance" given by the King?

All of the previous tasks are to be completed by the assigned time. Those who do not complete them will be required to take additional Chance Cards.

Appendix 6

World Banquet Information and Chance Cards

Poverty Simulation
World Banquet Discussion Information

World Population by 2009 projected to be 6,872,820,423

LATIN AMERICA—
population approximately 548,500,000

Ask what they ate and where they are from. Then, ask them to name some countries (Venezuela, Columbia, Ecuador, Peru, Bolivia, Chile, Brazil, Paraguay, Uruguay, Guyana, Suriname, French Guiana, Trinidad, Panama, Guatemala, Honduras, El Salvador, Mexico, Costa Rica, Nicaragua, Belize).

What are three of the larger cities in the world?

Mumbai (Bombay), India	11,914,398	2001c
Shanghai, China	10,996,500	2003e
São Paulo, Brazil	10,927,985	2005e

Source: Eternal Perspective Ministries, www.epm.org

Tokyo, Japan's population in 2005, according to United Nations reports was more than 35 million people! Depending on which sources you consult and boundary lines you use, Mexico City's population ranges between 8 and 30 million people, and continues to increase. New York is at 8 million, but in 20 years, New York won't even be in the top ten.

According to some estimates, São Paulo, Brazil, has more than 10,000 street kids roaming the streets of downtown. They have formed their own culture, which is ruthless. São Paulo also has hundreds of shantytowns (or slums), called *favelas*, lining the streets for miles. These are sometimes right next to corporate high-rises where the kids who go to dumps to scavenge for food and other necessities can look and see men and women dressed in $100 suits and going to work.

Now, the US has poured millions into the Brazilian economy because we don't want the international recession to get any closer to us, but where do you think the money has gone? Into the corporations.

We think that if the Brazilian corporate world will recover and grow, then it will trickle down to these street kids. More than likely, it will not. And even if it doesn't, the street kids will not determine our foreign and economic policy toward Brazil.

What are some of the problems?

Let's talk about poverty and hunger—caused by *cash cropping*. Most farmers work fields with crops so that they can eat what is not sold or is left over. *Cash cropping* grows such things as tobacco, soybeans, coffee, and sugarcane. This has brought more profits but, when there is natural disaster, farmers neither have money from the profits to buy food nor the food, because their land has been used for no-food or cash crops.

We in the US have a major part to play in this, because these are crops we buy. When one corporation decides to employ farmers from other countries because it will be cheaper, it is because of the US market. What should we do? Check out www. ncccusa.org and read how Tony Campolo's class bought stock in a corporation working in the Dominican Republic.

Lastly, **what is the predominant religion in Latin America?** Catholicism. But what has recently emerged in the last 20 years? Charismatic movement.
• There is revival going on in Argentina.
• They are sending missionaries to places all over the world.
• Their biggest outreach is in Europe and the US.

AFRICA—population approximately 890,000,000
Ask what they ate and where they are from.
Ask them to name the topographical boundary between the

north and the south (Sahara). Southern countries are South Africa, Botswana, Namibia, Mozambique, Zimbabwe, Madagascar, Malawi, Zambia, Angola, Tanzania, Congo, Zaire, Gabon, Uganda, and Kenya.

Name some problems specific to the southern region of Africa.

AIDS.

- Twenty-eight million people in Africa are suffering from AIDS.
- (The population of New York City is 8 million and the population of Mumbai is almost 12 million.)

Another problem is poverty. And poverty leads to what other problem?

The problem of hunger

- Thirty-five thousand children die every day due to preventable diseases.
- They do not die of starvation, but rather, what? Undernourishment.
- You'll see babies eating sugarcane or other foods, but they are not getting the right vitamins and nutrients that their bodies need to function. Malnutrition causes a child's hair to turn red, their eyes to be crossed, and their stomachs to be bloated (like we see in the commercials).
- What's the number one killer of these children? Diarrhea, which costs a few cents to cure.
- What's the necessary caloric intake for each person? 2,000–2,200 a day.
- What is the average caloric intake for an American? 3,700.

Let's talk about poverty.

About 1.4 billion people (one-fourth) in the world are absolute poor, which means they do not make enough to meet their basic needs of food, clothing, and shelter.

What is the poorest country in the world (GNP)? Chad.

What is the poorest country in our hemisphere? Haiti.
Their average yearly income is $75.

What is the predominant religion in the southern region of Africa? Christianity.

But what is interesting is that when Christianity came, it replaced tribal religions.

Tribal religions, or most folk religions, deal with daily questions such as why there is a drought, or why there is sickness. High religions (Islam, Christianity, and Hinduism) deal with eternal questions such as where man came from and what heaven is like.

Which do you think tribal people will deal with daily?

Tribal questions. They may adopt a High religion, but they deal with their problems through their tribal beliefs. We call mixing these two religions together *syncretism*.

Now, name some countries in the northern region of Africa. (Ethiopia, Somalia, Sudan, Chad, Morocco, Niger, Mali, Algeria, Libya, Egypt, Senegal, Sierra Leone, Liberia, Ivory Coast, Togo, Ghana, Benin, Cameroon, Tunisia, and Eritrea.)

What is the predominant religion in the northern region? Islam.

We have a wrong perception of Muslims: that they have swords and their hair flowing in the air while riding on a camel. Most Muslims are warm and loving people. But we shouldn't forget as well that in the world today more Christians have been persecuted and martyred in this generation than in all previous generations put together. While the source of this persecution varies, much of it comes from Islamic Fundamentalist groups who see Christianity as a heretical distortion of the Old Testament. Human rights watch groups have targeted about 30 countries in the world, with 9 in Africa (Tunisia, Equatorial Guinea, Somalia, Morocco, Mauritania, Sudan, Nigeria, Egypt, and Libya). We need to be more active in raising awareness of this part of the body of Christ.

Let's talk about Islam.

Muhammad lived from 570–632. He married young and worked alongside his first wife, who was a wealthy businesswoman, named Khadija. Because of her wealth, he was allowed the privilege to search and seek out spiritual yearnings. He left home to meditate in a cave and is said to have been visited by an angel who gave him the word of God. This word eventually became the Koran. He said the revelations came over several years and, as he shared his visions, people became converted. His first convert was his wife.

In 622, because of the many conversions, he was kicked out of Mecca by the ruling elite class, and so it was the poor and marginalized that started to follow him. He went to Medina and built his following. There, for the first time, his religion was given a name, Islam. A follower of Islam, therefore, is called a Muslim, which means "one who is submitted to God." These followers were involved in battles and many of the men were killed. This left many widows to care for. So Muhammad encouraged the men to take in these widows to protect them. When Khadija died, Muhammad married again to Aissa, who was his beloved.

In 630 Mecca surrendered to Muhammad, and in 632 he died. This caused a problem, for there was really no plan for when and if he died. Therefore, much confusion reigned.

There are five tenets of Islam and they are:

1. the Shahada—there is no god but Allah and Muhammad is his prophet;
2. The Salat—pray five times daily;
3. Alms giving—Muslims give 2.5 percent of their disposable income;
4. Fast in the month of Ramadan—from sunup to sundown; and
5. The Hajj—a pilgrimage to Mecca.

Let's talk about the differences between Islam and Christianity.

Muslims believe that Adam was the first Muslim, and that Jews, Christians, and all people are actually Muslims, but that we have strayed. They also don't believe that Adam's sin affected all people, just Adam. So, they believe in the innate goodness in all people. Therefore, they have a hard time understanding our concept of the Trinity. And they disagree with our belief that God had a Son, and that Jesus was both human and divine; they think we have exaggerated His importance. They question why we need a Savior if we are not born in sin?

They think Christians mistakenly think that Jesus is equivalent to Muhammad. The equivalent of Jesus to a Muslim is the Koran. They believe that the Koran is only God's word when read in Arabic, and they believe that the reading of the Koran brings great blessings on one's life.

Let's talk about the two kinds of Islam. What are they?

Sunni and Shiite.

Which has the greater number of followers? Sunni. And where are Sunni followers found? Iran.

Where are Shiite followers found? Iraq.

What is the largest Islamic country in the world? Indonesia.

Where is the second largest population of Muslims? Pakistan.

Historically, Jews, Christians, and Muslims all got along (for example, the Turks provided shelter for Jews in the eighth or ninth century), but later came the genocide of Armenian Christians.

Abraham had two sons: Ishmael and Isaac. Ishmael's sons were Muslims; Isaac's sons were Jews. During the Crusades. Christians, with a cross on their chest, killed Muslims in the name of Christ. This is still remembered among most Muslims.

Islam is the fastest-growing non-Christian religion in the world. And yet how many Christian missionaries are working primarily among Muslims? Less than 6 percent. The following chart reflects the distribution of Protestant missionaries among cultural groups in 2000, according to a statistical article posted by www.thetravelingteam.org:

74%	**Among Nominal Christians**
8%	**Among Tribal Peoples**
6%	**Among Muslims**
4%	**Among Nonreligious/Atheists**
3%	**Among Buddhists**
2%	**Among Hindus**
2%	**Among Chinese Folk Religions**
1%	**Among Jewish Peoples**

Source: Eternal Perspective Ministries, www.epm.org

It takes about seven years in relationship with Christians for a Muslim to understand the love of Christ and Christianity.

South Asia—India—population approximately 1,600,000,000

- Ask what they ate and where they are from.
- India is such a huge country we treat it by itself, 1 billion people.
- There are literally people everywhere.
- What is the country to the west? Pakistan (Muslim).
- To the east? Nepal and Bangladesh.
- To the south? Sri Lanka. To the north? Tibet.
- How do you eat? With your right hand, because your left hand is used for cleaning yourself. In this culture it is very offensive to touch someone with your left hand. It is thought, *Why would you go into a dark room and save that stuff on paper?*
- What is the primary religion of India? Hinduism.

Let's talk about Hinduism.

The original inhabitants of India were the Dravidians. There was an Aryan invasion (these are not the Germans, but from the Caspian Sea) in 1500 B.C., and their original belief system began a lot of Hindu thought. They began the sacrificial system (of animals) and they created the caste system. (The name for the caste system is *Varna*, which means "color." Sound familiar?)

The basic castes are:
- Brahmins—Priests
- Kshatriya—Warriors, military
- Vaishya—Merchants
- Shudra—Tillers of the land
- Harijans—Untouchables; they handled sewers and dead carcasses

This started out as a kind of feudal system, and then was used as a means of order. It became institutionalized and oppressive. This still is a means not of vocation, but of social control. Culturally you marry only in your caste.

Another phase in the growth of Hinduism is the development of scripture, called the Upanishads in 3 B.C. This is similar to our Reformation with Martin Luther. The writers of these were tired of the heavy burden caused by the Brahmins and the sacrificial system; so, they developed the idea of the Atman, belief that the true self is within each of us—that each of us has the divine within us. The focus of the religion went from the power of the priesthood and the magic prayer to the Ultimate Reality. And each of us is supposed to have some of the Ultimate Reality within us. The name of the Ultimate Reality is the *Brahman* (notice the spelling difference). What determines whether we move closer to Brahman or not is our *karma*. When our karma is not good, we are locked into Samsara, which is reincarnation. Karma determines what caste you are born into.

Karma is able to express the injustice in life. Example: the beggar dying in the streets. The goal of all of life is to achieve *moksha*, which is release from samsara.

When we achieve moksha, our Atman has become one with Brahman, like a drop of water falling into the ocean.

Brahman is what all things flow from and to. All things come from Brahman and all things go to Brahman; that is why it is wrong to kill living things. Brahman is essentially an impersonal existence, and so, to become one with Brahman, we must lose what keeps us from moksha, which is desire.

If we can quench all desire, through meditation, chanting, or whatever, then we can move into moksha, and lose ourselves into an impersonal existence.

One last thing about Hinduism. As we look at Hinduism, we see that adherents worship up to 3 million gods. Some devout Hindus say that there is only one god who is called Brahma, and the rest of these gods are incarnations of him. He then is also known as Krishna, Vishnu, Shiva, Rama, Lakshmi, and others. These are incarnations, or *avatars* of him.

Christianity makes up about 2 percent of India's population. Only 1 percent is in the north, which is a part of the 10/40 Window where 80 percent of all unreached people live.
Do you know how many missionaries work among Christians or nominal Christians? The answer is staggering and should shoot off like fireworks!

74%	**Among Nominal Christians**
8%	**Among Tribal Peoples**
6%	**Among Muslims**
4%	**Among Nonreligious/Atheists**
3%	**Among Buddhists**
2%	**Among Hindus**
2%	**Among Chinese Folk Religions**
1%	**Among Jewish Peoples**

There is a group in northern India called the Gujjars. The Gujjars are seminomadic and live in the foothills of the Himalayas. Twenty years ago, there were no known believers in Issa (Jesus) among them. Now after 20 years of prayer, visits, persistence, and the presence of several godly couples, there are numerous new believers.

East Asia—China—population approximately 1,500,000,000
Ask what they ate and where they are from. Then, ask them to name some countries in Asia. (China, Laos, Cambodia,

Vietnam, Taiwan, Myanmar, Japan, North and South Korea, Philippines, Malaysia, Indonesia, and Mongolia) Let's primarily focus on China. One of out five people on the face of the earth is Chinese.

What is the largest city in China? Shanghai. Shanghai moved into second place, in the 2007 *Almanac*. What status did China try desperately to achieve? Most Favored Nation status. China was admitted to WTO in 2001, so they enjoy free international trade.

2 Shanghai, China	10,996,500	2003e

What previously kept them from that status? Their atrocious human rights history. They are among the 30 countries human rights groups have labeled with the greatest amount of persecution of Christians.

There are three streams of thought that make up the religious thought of China. China, first of all, is so huge that there cannot be one form of religion that all share. Predominantly, what are the three influences? Confucianism, Taoism, and Buddhism.

Confucianism's major influence is seen in the emphasis upon relationships within China. Confucius lived before the spread of Buddhism when China was largely a feudal state. Confucius mainly started out trying to ensure peace between warring parties. Confucianism is understood among the Chinese that for them to live at all is to live in relation to others. Humanity is not achieved then through conversion to a certain system of beliefs, but through entering into relationship with others.

As Confucianism focuses on the relationship aspect, Daoism focuses on the otherworldly aspects. As Confucius dealt with business and relationships, Daoism deals with the supernatural, with a heavy emphasis upon the deification of the natural. Dao is the path that the universe follows and all that it contains. Words cannot adequately describe Dao, as Dao is both above us and within and around us. It is both immanent or present and transcendent or beyond the present. Dao is best known in the symbols of the yin and the yang. These are the dual principles that are necessary and complementary for each other in order to maintain balance in the universe. Sickness, or other forms of evil, is thought to be caused by a disruption in the balance of the yin and the yang.

The third stream of thought is Buddhism. Buddhism, originated in the fifth-century B.C.E. and is 2,500 years old. It was started by Siddhartha Gautama, who lived in East India. His father was very wealthy and did not want him to see the pain and evil of this world. But throughout his life, Buddha snuck out to see sickness, death, and poverty among people. This formed his thought as he came to believe that we are all born into a world of suffering. Later in his life, he renounced his wealth, his wife, and son; and he became a wandering ascetic, seeking enlightenment. He tried many things as he sought happiness (that's why we see him as fat and as skinny), and finally he became frustrated and sat under a *Bodi* tree. There, he supposedly received enlightenment, and he began to teach what he called the Middle Path, which is eightfold.

The basis of this belief system is: all is misery and everything has a reason for it. If the cause can be destroyed, so can the effect. The path to destroy the cause is desire. Moksha, which in Hinduism is release into Brahma, is in Buddhism called *nirvana*. nirvana is the end of change and is complete union with Brahma. Desire only leads us away from nirvana, so it must be destroyed. Once more, there is an emphasis upon the loss of self into an ultimate impersonal existence.

Within Buddhism there are two main schools of thought: from the north is *Mahayana* and from the south *Theravada*. Theravada, which comes from primarily Cambodia and Thailand, has an emphasis upon reincarnation of the individual and ultimate union with the source of the universe. This ultimately spread to the US as Zen Buddhism. With Buddhism being popular in Asia, when did it spread to the US? The 1960s. What movement has this helped to spread? New Age. It has also been known here as Zen Buddhism and Hare Krishna. Two key figures in the spread of this were poets Jack Kerouac and Allen Ginsberg.

Europe—population approximately 710,000,000

Ask what they ate and where they are from. Ask participants to name some countries. (Spain, Portugal, England, France, Luxembourg, Germany, the Netherlands, Sweden, Denmark, Norway, Finland, Romania, Yugoslavia, Slovenia, Macedonia, Albania, Greece, Bulgaria, Bosnia-Herzegovina, Croatia, Hungary, Czechoslovakia, Poland, Belarus, Lithuania, Ukraine, Moldova, Italy, Switzerland, Belgium, Ireland, Latvia, Estonia, and Russia)

What is the predominant religion in Europe, according to students on the street? They would say that they are post-Christian or atheist. They have seen the affects of Christianity on their countries (the compromise of the German church of Nazism) and they do not see the difference made.

What is the fastest growing religion now in Europe? Islam. Cathedrals are being turned into mosques. People have said that whatever happens in Europe happens in the US 20 years later.

Another aspect of Europe we need to know about is happening in the Balkans. Name some countries from the Balkans. (Macedonia, Yugoslavia, Slovenia, Bosnia, Albania, Bulgaria, and Croatia)

There are three basic religions in this area. What are they? Catholic, Orthodox Christian, and Muslim. Catholics are found among Serbs, Orthodox Christian are Croats, and Muslims are Albanians and Bosnians.

In the last several years we have seen so much conflict between these groups because of the fall of communism. Historically, this area has been under the domination of hostile countries, whether they are from Austria (Hapsburg) or Ottoman Empire (Turkey).

These groups have always hated each other, but their expression of hatred didn't flourish until they had achieved a measure of freedom. Their hatred is also founded upon endless historical conflicts that they see as having much relevance on the present. These conflicts are also more rooted in their nationalism than their religious beliefs, as much of their religion is mainly nominal. Why is this area important? It has been called the powder keg to Europe. (Remember World War One?)

North America—population approximately 514,000,000 (US population 300,000,000 as of 2006)

Ask what they ate and where they are from. Then, ask what feelings they had being at this table.

What religion best characterizes the US to the rest of the world? Christianity.

The US is the number one exporter of weapons and pornography to the rest of the world. In the past, one of the most watched TV programs in the world was *Baywatch*, and before that *Dallas*. No wonder, when Western Christians overseas say they are from the US, many nationals think that they are rich, greedy, and immoral.

There are 17 industrialized nations and among those what number is the US in the giving of foreign aid? Number 17. Number 1 is Sweden, and number 2 is Japan. What is one reason the US gives aid? To protect military sites. If we were interested in humanitarianism, then why didn't we invade South Africa for the last 30 years?

Ask the rest of the people what they felt about the Americans.

As Christians, should we feel responsible? Yes. Because responsibility produces change, which affects what we choose or choose not to consume when the rest of the world is going hungry.

The cultural institutionalized organizations that we label religious seem to be a far cry from the body of Christ that Jesus founded and the Holy Spirit equipped and unleashed for ministry. What if the church of today got ahold of the vision to reach the world, to reach the cities, and to reach the poor of the world for Christ? Would it change the way we do things?

How do we bring together the passion for Christ and passion for the poor? Tony Campolo says that the two are to be brought together; that not only could they go together, *but they must be together.*

There is a word you should know about—*justice*. Justice is our relationship with others. We have thought for too long that we could love the Lord with all our hearts and then go and do anything we wanted. But justice has two words in the Old Testament, *daqah* and *mishpat*, which ultimately mean the same thing as *righteousness*. *Justice* and *righteousness* are interchangeable.

In Matthew when Jesus says that the first commandment is to love God, and the second is like it, means that the second has the same weight. If we claim to love God outside of our loving the poor, then our love for Him is empty at best. At worst, our love is a lie.

If someone has to look at your wrist or see a cross around your neck to see what you believe, and they can't tell it from your actions, then, according to James, your faith is dead. When we get to heaven, God is not going to ask us about our doctrine. He is going to ask us if we fed the hungry, clothed the naked, and visited the sick and imprisoned. And what will you tell Him?... I do want to know if you accepted Christ as your Lord in the fourth grade, and I also want to know how you live with Christ as your Lord today. The world can tell by your actions towards the ones with whom He identifies: the poor.

Global Population Percentages

Note: *South Asia, East Asia, Latin America, and Africa sit on the floor. Europe and North America in chairs and tables. All decorated to fit cultural theme.*

South Asia: 29% x number of participants
Menu: Curry and rice, chapatti, and chai
> Three cups raw rice per eight people; serve in bowls, chapati on top
> Chai—hot tea with sugar, creamer, and cardamom

East Asia: 27% x number of participants
Menu: Fried rice, hot tea, and chopsticks
> Three-quarters cup fried rice in bowl, and black tea

Latin America: 8% x number of participants
Menu: Tamales or burritos, black or pinto beans, corn tortillas, and coffee

Africa/Middle East: 16% x number of participants
Menu: Small portions of roast chicken, sweet potatoes, flat bread, and tap water
> On round tray put one piece of flat bread per person with drained sweet potatoes and small unidentifiable pieces of chicken to share.

Note: *Europe and North America sit at tables with tablecloths and nice place settings.*

Europe: 14% x number of participants
Menu: German sausage, potato salad, slaw, rolls, and grape juice
> Heat sausage in skillet.

North America: 6% x number of participants
Menu: Steak, baked potato, salad, dessert, iced tea, water, coffee
> Salad in bowl first with dressing of choice, course by course
> Extremely large, beautiful ice-cream sundae

World Banquet Shopping List

Saturday Breakfast:
___ Cheap soft drinks
___ Cheap chips

World Banquet:
(*—item in more than one country or needed elsewhere during the simulation)

USA .06

☐ Steak
☐ Baked potatoes
☐ Bacon bits
☐ Sour cream
☐ Grated cheese*
☐ Butter*
☐ Rolls*
☐ Salad*

☐ Salad dressings*
☐ Tea*
☐ Coffee*
☐ Water
☐ Ice cream
☐ Whipped cream
☐ Chocolate topping
☐ Vegetable (green)

Europe and Eurasia .14

☐ German sausage
☐ Potato salad
☐ Cole slaw
☐ Rolls*

☐ Grape juice
☐ Coffee*
☐ Apple strudel
☐ Water

Latin America .08

☐ Tamales, burritos
☐ Canned black beans

☐ Corn tortillas
☐ Thick coffee*

East Asia .27

☐ Fried rice 1 box per 14 people
☐ Hot tea*

South Asia–India .29

- [ ] Roasted chicken
- [ ] Rice(3 cups raw per 12 people)
- [ ] Cooking oil for the curry
- [ ] Curry
- [ ] Ginger for the curry
- [ ] Tomatoes for the curry
- [ ] Onions for the curry
- [ ] Cayenne pepper for the curry
- [ ] Tortillas* (2 per person)
- [ ] Hot tea*
- [ ] Cardamom for the tea
- [ ] Cream for the tea
- [ ] Sugar for the tea

Africa/Mideast .16

- [ ] Flat bread or tortillas* (2 per person)
- [ ] Roasted chicken from deli
- [ ] Sweet potatoes

Chance Cards Apples

- [ ] Apples (1 per person plus 10)

Sunday Breakfast:

- [ ] Waffles (2 per person)
- [ ] Butter*
- [ ] Small link sausage
- [ ] Syrup
- [ ] Orange juice* 1 gal for 10 people

Sunday Lunch:

- [ ] Lasagna (1 large per 12 people)
- [ ] French bread (1 loaf per 8–10 people)
- [ ] Salad* (1 bag for 20 people)
- [ ] Butter*
- [ ] Salad dressing*
- [ ] Tea
- [ ] Ice-cream sandwiches

Appendix 7

Evaluation Form

Poverty Simulation Evaluation

Please answer the following questions honestly.
Your comments help us determine how to make the experience more meaningful for others.

1. How much money did you have left? $

2. Which four items did you select?
   (If homeless, check here: _____)
   a.
   b.
   c.
   d.

3. Rank in order of impact on you the following parts of the simulation (1 is highest impact):
   ☐ Welfare resources (money, four items, clothing, etc.)
   ☐ "Real-Life" Scavenger Hunt
   ☐ Church Under the Bridge
   ☐ Videos
   ☐ World Banquet
   ☐ Inner-city children's program
   ☐ Discussion and debriefing times
   ☐ Other (please explain): _____
   _____

4. In one statement, what do you understand now about poverty?
   _____
   _____
   _____

5. What do you think could be done to improve the learning

experience?

_____

_____

_____

6. Other thoughts or feelings about the experience.

_____

_____

_____

_____

Would you be interested in any of the following? Check those that apply.

☐ Summer Internship (age 19 or older; training)
☐ Mission Waco internship (age 18 or older; summer and/
 or school year)
☐ Out-of-country mission/exposure trips:
☐ Mexico City
☐ Haiti (18 or older)
☐ India (18 or older)
☐ Having a Mission Waco staff member speak to your
 church, student group, or organization
☐ Financially supporting Mission Waco
☐ Receiving the Mission Waco newsletter

*Name:*_____

*Age:*_____ *Phone:*_____

*Email:*_____

*Address:*_____

*City, State:*_____ *ZIP:*_____

*Group you came with:*_____

_____ *Today's date:* _____

The following card will be distributed on the second night for the participant to begin thinking about and writing down his or her commitments. They should be collected on the final morning (or no later than the evaluation time). Be sure that each student writes his or her address on the front. Mail these six to eight weeks after the Poverty Simulation experience.

A note to myself!

During the Mission Waco Poverty Simulation, I was challenged to understand God's concern for the poor and marginalized in the US and the world. I learned the following things that I want to remember:

_____

_____

_____

Today's date: _____

I am making some practical decisions about how to respond to the needs of the poor that I want to keep myself accountable to do when I get home. They include the following:

_____

_____

_____

If I forget or neglect these commitments, when I receive this card to myself, I will begin again to do them.

Signed:

Appendix 8
Resources for Content

I. **Worldviews:** The following information is very basic. The facilitator may want to find additional books, Web sites, and studies to become better informed. The information provided is based on our past and current research, including review of the sources cited in this guidebook's bibliography and additional resources. You may want to update this information with those and other sources.

   The goal is not to understand everything about each worldview, but to help stretch participants to understand the basic precepts, numbers of people who adhere to each worldview, how they view suffering, and the unique challenges each poses to the Christian worldview.

   A. **Hinduism** There are 1 billion Hindu, with 890 million in India)—millions of gods represented by idols; concept of karma and reincarnation; cause and effect. Poor are poor because of their own previous lifestyle. Helping others is primarily for one's own personal advancement.
   B. **Buddhism** (Central and Southeast Asia)—250 million; suffering (including poverty) comes from desire, so we must rid desire by the Four Noble Truths/Noble Eightfold path.
   C. **Islam** (Indonesia, North Africa, Middle East; Europe)—More than 1 billion; fastest growing non-Christian world religion; poor are poor because "Allah wills it." They give generously to the poor as one of the Five Pillars of Islam.
   D. **Animism,** also tribalism; spiritism (Southern Africa and other primitive cultures)—the spirit world is real and must be appeased; ancestral worship, curses, demons/angels, witchcraft, and so forth. Poor because the spirits are mad.

E. **Postmodernity/Atheist/Agnostic** (Europe)—second largest non-Christian worldview; many say "post-Christian."

F. **Pentecostalism** (Latin America)—a denomination of Christianity which focuses on supernatural, spiritual warfare and speaking in tongues; now larger than the Catholic church in South America; fastest growing Christian group; liberation theology also significant in Latin America

G. **Christianity**—2.1 billion; largest worldview; shrinking in the West, while growing in exponential ways in Asia, Latin America, and Africa. No one answer about why people are poor.

II. Global Social Concerns: While there are numerous and often complicated issues of social injustice, the goal of the facilitator is to help paint a broad sweep of concerns in which Christians should be actively involved. The continent or country in parentheses may be used in the discussion to highlight such problems. There are numerous Web sites, articles, books, and DVDs available on these.

A. Hunger (Southern Africa; Chad, Ethiopia)
B. Civil War/Militarism/Unjust Governments (Somalia)
C. Inadequate Health Care (Africa)
D. Racial Reconciliation
E. HIV/AIDS (Africa)
F. Cash-Cropping (Latin America)
G. Overpopulation (China)
H. Child Labor (India)
I. Sex Trade—Slavery (Thailand)
J. Environmental Problems (Haiti)

Statistics
Women and Children of the World

(The following data was compiled from UN sources by Women's Feature Service. Another resource is the World Health Organization.)

- Heterosexual transmission is the leading cause of HIV for women. Worldwide, 3,000 women are infected daily with the virus that causes AIDS.
- Of the estimated $2 billion spent annually on AIDS prevention, only about 10 percent is spent in the developing world, where 85 percent of infections occur.
- Eighty five million to 114 million women and girls have undergone female genital mutilation worldwide; each year an estimated 2 million more girls suffer the practice in Africa and Asia or as immigrants or refugees in Europe and North America.
- Maternal mortality rates have nearly halved since 1970, yet approximately 500,000 women still die from causes related to pregnancy and childbirth every year, 1,500 every day.
- A woman's risk of dying in childbirth in a developing country is 1 in 25 to 40, compared with 1 in 3,000 in developed countries.
- It is estimated that one-fourth of women worldwide are physically battered.
- In India, 6,200 dowry deaths were reported in 1994—or an average of 17 married women were killed daily for failure to make dowry payments to the husband's family.
- More than 20 million people have died of AIDS since 1981.
- Africa has 12 million AIDS orphans.
- By December 2004, women accounted for 47 percent of all people living with HIV worldwide, and for 57 percent in sub-Saharan Africa.
- Young people (15 to 24 years old) account for half of all new HIV infections worldwide—more than 6,000 become infected with HIV every day.

- Of the 6.5 million people in developing and transitional countries who need life-saving AIDS drugs, fewer than 1 million are receiving them.

Local Statistics

(The following data was compiled from the US Census for data in Waco.)

The City of Waco population is approximately 113,726. The best data available is 2000 census (compiled by the Texas State Data Center) which reports Anglo, African American, Hispanic, and other income for 1999. You may want to research and compile data for your city by accessing the most recent US Census.

- White, not Hispanic population 51.1 percent
- Black population 22.6 percent
- Hispanic population (any race) 23.6 percent
- Average household income $26,264
- Average family income $33,919
- Per capita income $14,584
- Median earnings for male $26,902
- Median earnings for female $21,159
- Percent of population below poverty 26.3 percent
- Related children under 18 in poverty 30.9 percent
- Age 65 and over in poverty 13.0 percent
- Percent of families in poverty 19.3 percent
- Number of households with income below $10,000 8,642 (20.4 percent)
- Number of households with income $10,000 to $14,999 4,412 (10.5 percent)
- Number of households with income $15,000 to $24,999 7,184 (17.0 percent)

(Total households in the census sample: 42,279
An additional Web site for this kind of information is:
http://txsdc.utsa.edu/)

According to http://www.aecf.org:

- Thirty-one percent of children are below the poverty line.
- Sixty-four percent are below 200 percent of poverty line
- Sixty percent live in high-poverty neighborhoods (where 20 percent or more of the population is below poverty)
    - Racial breakdown:
        - Forty percent are Hispanic
        - Forty one percent are African American
        - Seventeen percent are Anglo

Example 1: Texas Subsidized Apartment Complex Research

200 Units	850 Residents
182 Single women	1 Married
650 Under age 18	17 Elderly
0 Single men	

32 women living in this apartment complex surveyed

30—mothers	2—no children
9—high school	5—GED
3—Some junior college	

30 mothers had 87 children

People with Disabilities and Their Housing

A 2004 nationwide study shows that people with disabilities are paying an average of 109 percent of their monthly Supplemental Security Income (SSI) income to rent a modest one-bedroom apartment and 96 percent to rent an efficiency at fair market value. The study, Priced Out in 2004, was published by the Technical Assistance Collaborative and the Consortium for Citizens with Disabilities Housing Task Force (CCD).

"In this booming housing market, people with disabilities who rely on SSI payments are left further and further behind. Every year, rents for efficiencies and one-bedroom apartments far exceed the incomes for low-income individuals with disabilities," said Ann O'Hara, Technical Assistance Collaborative Housing Center associate director and study coauthor.

In 2004, the monthly income of a person with a disability on federal SSI benefits was $564 while the national average monthly rent for efficiencies or one-bedroom apartments was raised to their highest level ever—an average $676 for a one-bedroom rental. Overall, housing affordability has worsened significantly for SSI recipients. Since 1998, the amount of monthly SSI income needed to rent a modest one-bedroom unit has risen 59 percent—from 69 percent of SSI in 1998 to 109.6 percent of SSI in 2004.

For a copy of the report, which includes policy recommendations and state-level analyses, see: www.tacinc.org.

Each day, 30,000 children die from preventable deaths due to extreme poverty.

There are enough resources to stop this horrific reality, but the lack of moral and political will is simply not there for most Christians. (In 2007, World leaders will gather during the opening of the United Nations General Assembly to review commitments made by 140 nations in 2000 to cut global poverty by one-half by the year 2015. This type of meeting provides us a great time to be reminded and to do something.)

Would you consider...

1. Writing a note to the President or your congressman to encourage the United States to be a part of that effort?
2. Praying (and fasting) for the children on one of those days as an act of solidarity and reminder of the plight of millions?
3. Bringing a special offering to the annual Mission Waco Walk for the Homeless, that will be given to various groups who work with global poverty?

Global Statistics—Poverty—Facts and Statistics

According to http://www.globalissues.org:

Half the world—nearly 3 billion people—live on less than $2 a day.

- The GDP (Gross Domestic Product) of the poorest 48 nations (i.e., a quarter of the world's countries) is less than the wealth of the world's three richest people combined.
- Nearly a billion people entered the twenty-first century unable to read a book or sign their names.
- Less than 1 percent of what the world spent every year on weapons was needed to put every child into school by the year 2000 and yet it didn't happen.
- Fifty-one percent of the world's 100 wealthiest bodies are corporations.
- The wealthiest nation on Earth has the widest gap between rich and poor of any industrialized nation.
- The poorer the country, the more likely it is that debt repayments are being extracted directly from people who neither contracted the loans nor received any of the money.
- Twenty percent of the population in the developed nations consumes 86 percent of the world's goods.
- The top fifth of the world's people in the richest countries enjoy 82 percent of the expanding export trade and 68 percent of foreign direct investment—the bottom fifth, barely more than 1 percent.
- In 1960, the 20 percent of the world's people in the richest countries had 30 times the income of the poorest 20 percent—in 1997, 74 times as much.
- An analysis of long-term trends shows the distance between the richest and poorest countries was about:

  - 3 to 1 in 1820
  - 11 to 1 in 1913
  - 35 to 1 in 1950
  - 44 to 1 in 1973
  - 72 to 1 in 1992

- "The lives of 1.7 million children will be needlessly lost this year [2000] because world governments have failed to reduce poverty levels"
- The developing world now spends $13 on debt repayment

for every $1 it receives in grants.

- A few hundred millionaires now own as much wealth as the world's poorest 2.5 billion people.
- "The 48 poorest countries account for less than 0.4 per cent of global exports."
- "The combined wealth of the world's 200 richest people hit $1 trillion in 1999; the combined incomes of the 582 million people living in the 43 least developed countries is $146 billion."
- "Of all human rights failures today, those in economic and social areas affect by far the larger number and are the most widespread across the world's nations and large numbers of people."
- "Approximately 790 million people in the developing world are still chronically undernourished, almost two-thirds of whom reside in Asia and the Pacific."
- According to UNICEF, 30,000 children die each day due to poverty. And they "die quietly in some of the poorest villages on earth, far removed from the scrutiny and the conscience of the world. Being meek and weak in life makes these dying multitudes even more invisible in death." That is about 210,000 children each week, or just under 11 million children under five years of age, each year.
- For economic growth and almost all of the other indicators, the last 20 years [of the current form of globalization, 1980–2000] have shown a very clear decline in progress as compared with the previous two decades [1960–1980]. For each indicator, countries were divided into five roughly equal groups, according to what level the countries had achieved by the start of the period (1960–1980). Among the findings:
- Growth: The fall in economic growth rates was most pronounced and across the board for all groups or countries.
- Life Expectancy: Progress in life expectancy was also reduced for four out of the five groups of countries, with

the exception of the highest group (life expectancy 69–76 years).

- Infant and Child Mortality: Progress in reducing infant mortality was also considerably slower during the period of globalization (1980–1998) than over the previous two decades.
- Education and literacy: Progress in education also slowed during the period of globalization.
- "Today, across the world, 1.3 billion people live on less than one dollar a day; 3 billion live on under two dollars a day; 1.3 billion have no access to clean water; 3 billion have no access to sanitation; 2 billion have no access to electricity."
- The richest 50 million people in Europe and North America have the same income as 2.7 billion poor people. "The slice of the cake taken by 1 percent is the same size as that handed to the poorest 57 percent."
- The world's 497 billionaires in 2001 registered a combined wealth of $1.54 trillion, well over the combined gross national products of all the nations of sub-Saharan Africa ($929.3 billion) or those of the oil-rich regions of the Middle East and North Africa ($1.34 trillion). It is also greater than the combined incomes of the poorest half of humanity.
- A mere 12 percent of the world's population uses 85 percent of its water, and these 12 percent do not live in the Third World.

According to UNICEF:
- 1.2 billion people live on less than $1 a day
- every day, 800 million people go to bed hungry, and
- every day, 28,000 children die from poverty-related causes.

Consider the global priorities in spending in 1998

Global priorities in spending in 1998	
Global Priority	$US Billions
Basic education for everyone in the world	6
Cosmetics in the United States	8
Water and sanitation for everyone in the world	9
Ice cream in Europe	11
Reproductive health for all women in the world	12
Perfumes in Europe and the United States	12
Basic health and nutrition for everyone in the world	13
Pet foods in Europe and the United States	17
Business entertainment in Japan	35
Cigarettes in Europe	50
Alcoholic drinks in Europe	105
Narcotics drugs in the world	400
Military spending in the world	780

State of the Children
According to UNICEF, www.unicef.org:

- Number of children in the world: 2.2 billion
- Number in poverty: 1 billion (every second child)
- Shelter, safe water, and health: For the 1.9 billion children from the developing world, there are:
  - 640 million without adequate shelter (1 in 3)
  - 400 million with no access to safe water (1 in 5)
  - 270 million with no access to health services (1 in 7)

Children lacking education, worldwide—121 million
Survival for children worldwide:
- Ten million, six-hundred thousand died in 2003 before they reached the age of five (same as children population in

France, Germany, Greece and Italy)
- One million, four hundred thousand die each year from lack of access to safe drinking water and adequate sanitation.

Health of children worldwide:

- Two million two hundred thousand children die each year because they are not immunized.
- Fifteen million children orphaned due to HIV/AIDS (similar to the total children population in Germany or United Kingdom).
- The total wealth of the top 8.3 million people around the world "rose 8.2 percent to $30.8 trillion in 2004, giving them control of nearly a quarter of the world's financial assets." In other words, about 0.13 percent of the world's population controlled 25 percent of the world's assets in 2004.

Videos and Information About hunger and poverty:

Help and Hope (video)—InterVarsity Press
Compassion, International—
    www.compassion.com/TonyCampolovideo/
    or call 1-800-336-7676
World Vision—www.worldvision.org/video
Food for the Hungry
Make Poverty History (video)–Catholic Campaign for
    Human Development
Bread for the World
The Least of These (video)—Tony Campolo—
    www.christiancinema.com
Food First, "Twelve Myths About Hunger" (handout)
C.R.O.P. Hunger Walks

Biblical References
About God's Concern for the Poor

I. God created the world with enough resources for all creation and gave mankind the responsibility to oversee it.
  A. The Garden of Eden represents God's goodness and desire for us (Genesis 1–2).
  B. "The Cultural Mandate" calls us to subdue the earth (Genesis 1:28).
  C. God's intention is that there "be no poor among you" (Deuteronomy 15:4).

II. Sin entered into the world and its results have caused creation to "groan."
  A. Work became harder (Genesis 3:17–19).
  B. Families struggled; Cain killed Abel (Genesis 4:8).
  C. Injustices increased (Amos and other eighth-century prophets).

III. God provided guidelines for His people that would help overcome the systemic sins.
  A. Provisions for the poor to get food and assistance (Ruth—gleaning).
  B. Release from oppressive debt (Leviticus 25—Sabbath year and year of Jubilee).
  C. Fair treatment to the wanderer and stranger (Isaiah 58:7).

IV. God became frustrated with the religious hypocrisy and piety of outward religion that did not manifest itself in concern for one's neighbor. He ultimately brought punishment on the children of Israel for their "double-minded" ways.
  A. "The kind of fasting I have chosen is to loose the chains of injustice . . . set the oppressed free . . . share your

food with the hungry, and clothe the naked" (Isaiah 58:6–12), [paraphrase of NIV].

B. The Pharisees were very religious people but their religion was self-centered and condemned by Jesus.

V. Messiah was prophesied to be one who cared for the poor and oppressed.

A. "Preach good news to the poor" (Isaiah 61:1–4; fulfilled in Luke 4:18–19 by Jesus).

B. John's disciples confirmed Jesus was Messiah because He cared for them (Luke 7:18–22).

C. He spent time with the leper, the prostitute, the sick, and the hated tax collector.

D. We are to be "followers" of Jesus and do those same things.

VI. True faith cares for one's neighbors and the disenfranchised.

A. "Love the Lord . . . and your neighbor as yourself" (neighbor = person in need) (Matthew 22:37–40).

B. "Whatever you did for one of the least of these brothers of mine you did it for me" (Matthew 25:40).

C. "True religion . . . cares for orphans and widows" (James 1:27).

D. "If anyone has material possessions and sees his brother in need but has not pity on him, how can the love of God be in him?" (1 John 3:17).

VII. Wealth and riches blind us from God's truth and desires (rich young ruler).

A. The "rich fool" (Luke 12:13–21)

B. The "rich young ruler" (Luke 18:18–30)

C. The conversion of Zaccheus included repentance and redistribution of his wealth.

VIII. The church is a sign of the kingdom of God now and in the future.

    A. "Your kingdom come, your will be done on earth as it is in heaven" (Matthew 6:10).

    B. "Remember the poor" (Galatians 2:10), Paul was reminded by the Jerusalem church.

    C. The early church met each other's needs (Acts 2).

    D. The church took up collections for the poor.

    E. The "holistic" gospel calls us to make a difference in our own broken communities and "dark places" and "repair walls and streets" (Isaiah 58:12).

Source: *Sojourners* magazine, February/March 1974, www.sojo.net

Appendix 10

Chance Cards

Create small cards with these commands or write the words on
  popsicle sticks (for distribution after the World Banquet).

Friend needs gas - Pay facilitator $3

Emergency room fee - Pay facilitator $4

Found $3 in the thrift store coat pocket, get paid by
  facilitator

Toothache – Dentist fee $2 - Pay facilitator

Child has school project fee - $3- Pay facilitator

Need to buy Advil - $2 - Pay facilitator

Lost $3 – hole in pocket- Pay facilitator

Laundry - Pay facilitator $2

Paid friend for gasoline used to go to work- Pay facilitator $2

Charged - $4 for loitering - Pay facilitator

Buy medicine for skinned knee - $2 - Pay facilitator

Need a blanket - $2 - Pay facilitator

Found a wadded up $1 by dumpster, get paid by facilitator

Gave lunch money to friend - $5 -Pay facilitator

Caught in the rain – buy plastic pancho $2 - Pay facilitator

Won lottery money - $5, get paid by facilitator

Need allergy medicine - $4 - Pay facilitator

New thrift store clothes for child - $3 - Pay facilitator

Late fee - $2 - Pay facilitator

Help friend with bail charge - $5 - Pay facilitator

Work Uniform - $5 - Pay facilitator

Need toothbrush - $2 - Pay facilitator

Help friend with $2 for bus ticket - Pay facilitator

Need caffeine – buy coke $1 - Pay facilitator

Found 150 alum. Cans - $3, get paid by facilitator

Buy school supplies - $5 - Pay facilitator

samples

Chance

Found $3
in the thrift
store coat
pocket, get
paid by facilitator

Chance

Gave lunch
money
to friend - $5
-Pay facilitator

Chance

Won lottery
money
- $5, get
paid by
facilitator

Appendix 11
Additional Resources

A Theology As Big As the City by Ray Bakke

Bridging the Gap, Bryant L. Myers, Series Editor, MARC, a division of World Vision International

Children and Violence, The Washington Forum Perspectives on our Global Future – World Vision, 1995 Nine Parts of Desire: The Hidden World of Islamic Women by Geraldine Brooks

Empowering the Poor! Author: Linthicum, Dr. Robert Publisher: World Vision Resources. Category: Holistic Mission

Exploring World Mission, Bryan Myers, 2003 World Vision International

Great Religions of the World Encounter, Prepared by Midwest Center for Intercultural Studies, Chicago

Hard Living People and Mainstream Christians, Tex Sample (Abingdon, 1993), Islam, A Very Short Introduction, Malise Ruthven

Let Justice Roll Down by John M. Perkins,

Operation World by Patrick Johnstone and Jason Mandryk

Planting and Growing Churches, ed. Harvie M. Conn, Baker Books, 1997, p. 84 "World's Top Agglomeration"

Renewing The City: Reflections on Community Development And Urban Renewal by Robert D. Lupton

Street Children, A guide to Effective Ministry, Phyllis Kilbourn, editor, 1997 MARC Publications

The Pattern of New Testament Truth, Reprinted from George Eldon Ladd

Window on the World, Jill Johnstone, Daphne Spragget, 2001 Bethany House Publishing

Bibliography

Bread for the World www.bread.org.

CARE www.care.org.

Church Under the Bridge www.churchunderthebridge.org.

Compassion International www.compassion.com.

Dorrell, Janet C. "Inner City Subsidized Housing Research".
Mission Waco, 2002.

Dorrell, Jimmy. *Trolls and Truth: 14 Realities About Today's
Church That We Don't Want to See.* Birmingham, AL: New
Hope Publishers, 2006.

Dorrell, Jimmy M. "The Use of Experiential Learning as a
Primary Change Component for Understanding Differing
Sub-Cultures". Masters Diss., Baylor University, 1993.

Eternal Perspectives Ministry www.epm.org.

Faith Facts http://faithfacts.gospelcom.net.

Food and Agricultural Organization of the United Nations
www.fao.org.

Food for the Hungry www.fh.org.

Global Issues www.globalissues.org.

Global Missions status http://www.gordonconwell.edu.

The Heifer International www.heifer.org.

Keith-Lucas, Alan. *Giving and Taking Help.*: St. Davids, PA:
North American Association of Christians in Social Work;
revised March 1, 1994.

Kids Count Census Data Online http://www.aecf.org.

Kolb, David. *Experiential Learning: Experience as the
Source of Learning and Development.* Upper Saddle River,
NJ: Financial Times Press, 1983.

Mission Waco www.missionwaco.org.

National Center for Biotechnology Information
www.ncbigov.

National Coalition for the Homeless
www.nationalhomeless.org.

Peck, M. Scott. *The Different Drum: Community Making and
Peace.* New York, NY: Touchstone, 1998.

Population Reference Bureau www.prb.orgPublic Library and Digital Archive www.ibiblio.org.

Missions Statistics http://home.snu.edu.

Technical Assistance Collaborative www.tacinc.org.

Texas State Data center www.txsdc.utsa.edu.

UNICEF www.unicef.org.

U.S. Center for World Missions www.uscwm.org.

U.S. Census Bureau www.census.gov.

Voice of the Martyrs www.persecution.com.

wikipedia www.wikipedia.org.

Woman's Missionary Union www.wmu.com.

World Stats www.worldstats.org.

World Vision www.worldvision.org.

OTHER MINISTRY BOOKS

Street Signs
A New Direction in Urban Ministry
Ray Bakke and Jon Sharpe
ISBN 1-59669-004-6

Successful Mission Teams
A Guide for Volunteers
Martha VanCise
ISBN 1-59309-836-9

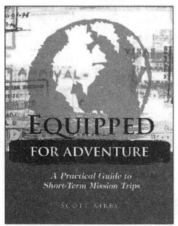

Equipped for Adventure
*A Practical Guide
to Short-Term Mission Trips*
Scott Kirby
ISBN 1-59669-011-9

Available in bookstores everywhere

For information about these books
or any New Hope product, visit
www.newhopepublishers.com.